I
BELIEVE
IN
LOVE

I
Believe
in
Love

Retreat Conferences on the Interior Life

Père Jean du Coeur de Jésus d'Elbée
OF THE CONGREGATION OF THE SACRED HEARTS

Translated from the French by
Marilyn Teichert, with Madeleine Stebbins
Both of C.U.F.

ST. BEDE'S PUBLICATIONS
Petersham, Massachusetts

I Believe in Love, Retreat Conferences on the Interior Life, by Père Jean du Coeur de Jésus d'Elbée, translated by Marilyn Teichert, with Madeleine Stebbins, from the original French edition, *Croire à L'Amour,* published in 1969 by Editions Saint Michel, Paris. Copyright © 1974 by Franciscan Herald Press, 1434 West 51st Street, Chicago, Illinois 60609. 1983 reprint of the above title by St. Bede's Publications by arrangement with Franciscan Herald Press.

Nihil Obstat: Mark Hegener, O.F.M.
       Censor Deputatus

Imprimatur: Msgr. Richard A. Rosemeyer, J.C.D.
       Vicar General, Archdiocese of Chicago

October 4, 1974

The Nihil Obstat and Imprimatur are official declarations that a book or pamphlet is free of doctrinal or moral error. No implication is contained therein that those who have granted the Nihil Obstat and Imprimatur agree with the contents, opinions, or statements expressed.

LIBRARY OF CONGRESS CATALOGING IN PUBLICATION DATA
Elbée, Jean du Coeur de Jésus d'.
  I believe in love.

  Translation of: Croire à l'amour.
  Reprint. Originally published: Chicago : Franciscan Herald Press, c1974.
  1. Spiritual life—Catholic authors. I. Title.
[BX2350.2.E413 1982]   248.4'82   82-24134
ISBN 0-932506-25-9 (pbk.)

COVER DESIGN BY M. ELIZABETH KLOSS, OSB

To
Mother Claire-Marie of the Heart of Jesus

Foreword

~~~~~~

To introduce this book to the reader, we quote a few words
of His Holiness Pope Paul VI about divine love and then
some words of praise from readers of the first edition.

In a discourse to a general audience on June 2, 1969, the
Holy Father spoke as follows:

"What is the discovery to which the man of faith comes
when he seeks the profound and complete sense of Divine
Revelation? This discovery is Love. God has above all revealed Himself as being Love. The whole history of salvation,
the whole Gospel is Love.

"We could quote so many pages of Scripture here. For
example, this one comes to mind:

'The Lord has appeared from afar to me. Yes, I have
loved you with an everlasting love: therefore have I drawn
you, taking pity on you' *(Jeremiah 31:3).*

"The whole epic of Redemption is Love and Mercy, the
effusion of the love of God upon us. And the history of
salvation is summarized in this well-known sentence of St.
Paul:

'That Christ may dwell by faith in your hearts: that,
being rooted and founded in charity, you may be able to
comprehend with all the saints, what is the breadth and
length and height and depth, to know also the charity of
Christ, which surpasses all knowledge: that you may be filled
unto all the fullness of God' *(Ephesians 3:17-19).*

"Let us stop here. We will have said enough about it
today in celebrating two feasts—of the Eucharist and of the
Sacred Heart—being so to speak driven by it toward the
prophetic point which presents them and lets us savor, if
not comprehend, something of their true religious sense, of
their superlative and violent reality: 'For God so loved . . .'

(John 3:16). And that moves us, overwhelms us. If we come
to the point of comprehending that we are loved to a supreme, unimaginable degree, unto silent, gratuitous, cruel
death, to the point of total immolation *(John, 19:30)* by him
whom we do not even know, or if we have known him, whom
we have denied and offended; if we come to the point of
comprehending that we are the objects of such a love, of so
great a love, we cannot remain complacent. . . .

"Such is the origin of the cult of the Sacred Heart of
Jesus: let us remember that the word heart is a symbol,
a sign, a synthesis of our Redemption viewed from the
divine and human interior life of Christ. Jesus loved us, the
Council tells us, equally 'with the heart of a man,' and how
much! Did you know that? Do you think about that? How
are you going to respond?"

To help us comprehend the love of God for us and to respond to it more fully is the purpose of the conferences
contained in this book.

That it can achieve this purpose is indicated by the following testimonies of some readers of the first French edition
who belong to every walk of life.

Cardinal Journet, Fribourg, December 17, 1969:
Thanking you profoundly for the beautiful little book and
for preaching the eternal truths with a heart forever new,
and asking the help of your prayers, Ch. Journet.

Prince Xavier de Bourbon-Parme, Paris, December 20, 1969:
I received your book, *Croire à l'Amour,* and I read it with
the feeling that I was hearing you speak.

In this time of uncertainty and anguish, when even many
Christians around us feel disoriented, your book is the great
answer. It is in the love of God which hovers over us that
we find the words of comfort for them and for ourselves.

Thank you with all my heart for having written this book.
It comes truly like grace from heaven, at its proper time,

bringing the joy of knowing better t ie goodness of the Lord, of approaching still nearer to him.

Jean Ladame, Superior of the Chaplains of Paray-le-Monial:
I am very touched by the honor you have done me in sending me your book. Here is true spiritual nourishment for souls, something that brings them into contact—I dare to say experimentally—with the burning Heart of Jesus. Souls are dying today because no one is nourishing in them the authentic mystical life. No one is steeping them in the living waters of salvation. Your book will be a revitalizing spring for them.

Mother Françoise-Thérèse of the Child Jesus, former Prioress of the Carmel of Lisieux:
I thank you for the grace which the reading of your book brought me. It is fully in the spirit of St. Thérèse of the Child Jesus. Yes, it is truly her message of "confidence and total abandonment" which is conveyed in it.

I am not surprised that souls are so comforted by it, so enlarged and drawn in the way of holiness. The Lord has given you the mission of making them believe in his love, and you fulfill it perfectly. That implies all the consequences it will have for the sanctification of souls, the eternal salvation of many.

A Professor of Dogmatic Theology:
I had the privilege and the joy of reading your Retreat. From a theological point of view, it is perfect, since you do nothing but explain—and with what authority and persuasion! —the Gospel.

It is of the highest quality, and it is the most fundamental of your works. The Sacred Heart cannot fail to bless it. He will make way for it and console many souls.

Some Members of Religious Orders:
(1) Thank you for your book. On each page I find what I need most: to believe in love and to abandon myself to this

all-surpassing love. You are right to say that confidence is not easy—that is, confidence without limits, confidence pushed to the point of "foolishness." But only this confidence is a worthy response of our hearts to the love of Our Lord

Now my difficulties no longer trouble me for I am sure of my Jesus. It is true that he hides himself, but at the same time it seems to me that nothing can separate us. I do not know how that is possible: nighttime in the soul and yet this sort of certainty that Jesus is very near; but since that helps me to love him more and more and unites me to him, I am very happy with everything he gives me.

(2) Without waiting any longer I want to thank you for your book, *Croire à l'Amour,* which is a delight and joy for me, and for my novices also. It helps me greatly to endure the numerous and varied trials which Jesus is permitting for me right now. I have said to "endure," but that is not the right word, for I believe rather that I "embrace" them with love, a love of the will at least, for my nature trembles. But as you say, that is normal, and Jesus, who knows our great weakness, understands it. Yes, with his grace, and thanks to you who have taught it to me, it has become easy for me always to say, "O Jesus, I thank you for everything."

A Youth Leader from the Society of St. Vincent de Paul:
Although very much preoccupied with reviewing for my exams, I have been discovering little by little Father d'Elbée's book. I have found in it the thing we need most in a tormented world like ours: serenity.

To believe in love is certainly the only reason to live, the only thing that gives sense to life. The Gospel of this morning said it again: "Greater love no man has than this: that he lay down his life for his friends."

You fear that the style is antiquated. But only the contingent goes out of fashion. Love, for its part, is eternally young, because it is never hardened into a mold, but always rushing like water, always stirring enthusiasm. Reading these pages I thought about other lines which you no doubt know, those of the marvellous Madeleine Delbrel: "If we truly loved you, Lord, we would know right away what dance it pleases you to have us dance, following the lead of your Providence."

In its way, your book also makes one want to dance.

Persons Living in the World:

(1) Thank you for having sent me *Croire à l'Amour*. The book is magnificent. This doctrine is my ideal, although unfortunately followed still at quite a distance. This life of faith, of abandonment, and of love has been the dream of my whole life! But the evening of our life does not escape the rule; like the evening of our days, it brings the dark, the loss of light. This little book will be a light in my night. The Holy Spirit has inspired you! I am deeply moved, and am going to make it my book for meditation.

(2) My daughter was in her agony for three days and three nights. I spent those days and nights with the little book, *Croire à l'Amour*, in my hands. I could not have endured those hours without it. I cannot keep to myself this discovery which I owe to you, and would like you to send this book to the following persons. . . .

(3) When I look for a word from Jesus, a desire of his Heart or himself, I open *Croire à l'Amour*. If you only knew how good it is to find him there and hear him speak to us, for he is there: you have put him into every line.

Thank you for this priceless gift.

Preface to the American Edition

My wife and I were introduced to this book while on a visit to France in 1971, and it made a deep impression on us both. It seemed then, as it seems now, to bring that nourishment for which the whole world is hungering: the divine love of the human Heart of Jesus for each single soul. In this little book, so full of the noblest and most tender sentiments, so devoid of any sentimentality, we see as if for the first time the unimaginable novelty of such familiar words as *God so loved the world . . . , Come unto Me . . . , This my son was dead, and is come to life again; was lost, and is found.*

In a gratefully astonished surrender to this love lies the seed of the renewal and reconciliation of which the world is in need and expectation. And it is worth remarking that this love, human and divine, this charism, this rushing spirit, this soaring flame, revisited the earth in a place hidden deep within the "structures of the institutional Church" which it is so fashionable to despise these days.

St. Thérèse of Lisieux is the principal teacher in this book; and no one could be a better target for much of the modern jargon. Where could one find anyone more deeply "buried in structure" than she? She was a small member in a small community of little nuns, locked behind their "medieval grille," weighed down by all kinds of "rules and regulations" which, we are now informed, effectively block all "fulfillment of personality!" St. Thérèse spent her short and glorious life in what the world can see only as a dark and lifeless cave; and there Love was born and lived and shone again, as in that night in Bethlehem, and that other night on Calvary.

It does not need special penetration to see that modern man has lost his way in his search for happiness, has alienated himself so profoundly from God that he has become alienated from himself, and is engaged in a sick and futile search for his own identity. What loneliness he suffers! A theme-song of desolation reverberates in his soul. He despairingly seeks guidance among those who are quite as lost as he is; and all his chosen guides lead him again to the same abyss from which there seems to be no way of return. In the end, suicide presents itself as the logical answer to those who choose this broad path—as modern literature and the newspapers bear witness.

This book comes like heavenly music, saving music, to fill with hope the emptiness of man's heart - and to fill it to overflowing.

I Believe in Love is a guide to happiness based on the teaching of one who found it entire: St. Thérèse of Lisieux. It is also a frame for a simple and universal program of spiritual renewal for the laity. God, through his Council, has announced unto us the universal vocation to holiness. If we reply in unconditional and loving confidence, "Behold the servants of the Lord; be it done to us according to your word," the result will be what it always is in such cases: Again and again the Word, having become flesh, will dwell among us. *Fiat!*

August, 1974   *H. Lyman Stebbins*
                                     Catholics United for the Faith

Contents

~~~~~~

Chapter 1

Love for Love

Pope Paul VI, addressing the members of the Congress on the Apostolate of the Laity on October 15, 1967, in St. Peter's, and wishing to summarize what lay spirituality must be, stated, "It will suffice to tell you in a word: only your personal and profound union with Christ will assure the fruitfulness of your apostolate, whatever it may be."

+ + +

During this retreat I intend to talk to you about confident love, following the teaching of St. Thérèse of Lisieux, of whom Pope Pius XII said, "she rediscovered the Gospel itself, the very heart of the Gospel."[1]

Could we imagine a stronger, more eloquent, more convincing affirmation of the divine depth of a doctrine? And this from the very mouth of the Pope, himself: "She has rediscovered the very heart of the Gospel."

I have entitled this first conference "Love for Love."

Prior dilexit nos (1 Jn 4:10); God loved us first that we might love him. That is the explanation of it all: of the Creation, the Incarnation, Calvary, the Resurrection, the Eucharist.

Creation, if we may express it in this way, is the infinite love which overflowed from him. God created us out of love for himself and out of love for his creatures whom he made in order to fill them with his love and his mercy. "It is because he is good that we are, that we exist," said St. Augustine. He did not create us out of necessity; he did not need us. He did not create us out of justice; he owed us nothing. No, it is to his sheer love that we owe our existence.

St. John the apostle who, while leaning on the breast of

1

Jesus in the Cenacle, perceived the beating of his heart and, at the same time, the secrets of his love, has revealed them all to us in his first epistle when he says,

Deus Caritas est: "God is love" *(1 Jn 4:8)*

God created us in the state of original justice, a marvelous state of equilibrium and harmony: our lower faculties perfectly subjected to our higher faculties, which were perfectly subjected to God. Then came the sin which upset all that, which deeply wounded our nature, which made us victims of concupiscence, of suffering, of sickness, of death.

Yet even so, God is so truly love itself that even before promulgating the punishment, he announced the Woman and her Son, victors over the serpent. If Adam had understood this, even before leaving the earthly paradise he would have been able to utter the astonishing cry of the Church on Holy Saturday: "Oh, truly necessary sin of Adam which was wiped out by the death of Christ! Oh, happy fault which merited such a Redeemer!"[2] *Felix culpa*, happy fault, which has meant for us so many sufferings, it is true, but so marvelous a Redemption!

And because God is Charity, he gave the world his beloved Son.

"For God so loved the world that he gave his only begotten Son" *(Jn 3:16)*.

That first sin, rejection of an infinite love, could not be repaired by any but an infinite love. The Word of God became incarnate in order that love might triumph in him and through him.

Jesus bought a twofold right on Calvary at the price of all his blood: the right, for him, to love us in spite of, or even because of our sins, our unworthiness; and the right, for us, to love him from the depths of our immense misery and to contemplate his divine attributes, including his justice, within his infinite mercy.

St. Paul, speaking of Calvary, finds only one phrase for this: "the folly of the Cross" *(1 Cor 18:23)*.

The Word became flesh and brought about all these mysteries, which we can summarize in a word: Bethlehem, Nazareth, Gethsemane, Calvary, the Eucharist—unfathomable abysses of that merciful love.

The Incarnation: the immense God whom heaven and earth cannot contain, a tiny infant lying on the hay in a manger; Nazareth: the life of God on earth for thirty years; a life of obedience, of poverty, of silence in total self-effacement. At Gethsemane he appears before his Father, covered with our sins, he, who "bore our sins in his body" *(1 Pt 2:24).* He obtains for us the right to appear one day before the Father covered with the blood flowing from every pore of his body under the pressure of his agony, and shed on Calvary to the last drop. Then the Father will not recognize us as sinners, but as his children, regenerated and renewed by the baptism of this blood; he will take us for his beloved Son.

See this sublime exchange: Jesus takes our sins upon himself and we make his merits our own. And the Father receives us as if we were his beloved Son, through infinite mercy, but in all justice.

After a retreat in which I had preached this with great conviction, a retreatant said to me, "I want most especially to retain one thought from your retreat: my sins on him, his blood on me."

In the hour of our agony, in that hour of truth, when, at the moment of our appearance before God, we perhaps review in our memory our whole life, with so many miseries and weaknesses, so many failings and falls, I hope that with contrite hearts but immense confidence we shall say to Jesus, "All this, all this I give you. Did you not come to earth to seek out my sins and take them upon yourself? In exchange, give me the price of your blood, the treasures of your Redemption, all your merits; they are mine."

It is in this spirit that little St. Thérèse said, "In the evening of this life I shall appear before you with empty hands."[3] "It is just this - to find myself at my death with

empty hands - that gives me joy, for having nothing I shall
receive everything from God."[4] What depth, what logic,
what refinement of love there is in these words!

All our spiritual wealth, all our supernatural goods, all our
life of holiness, all are Jesus and nothing but Jesus. He is
ours, his merits are ours, the price of his blood is ours, he
is completely ours.

"He delivered himself" *(Gal 2:20)* to us without reserva-
tion, that we might use him, that we might—I even dare to
say—abuse him. He wants to substitute himself in our lives
for everything on the condition, certainly, of our entire good
will in the gift of ourselves, about which I shall speak to
you again.

You understand here by what divine inspiration John
XXIII sought to revive in our hearts the devotion to the
Precious Blood of Jesus, uniting this to the cult of the Most
Holy Name of Jesus and of His Sacred Heart.[5]

After Gethsemane came the horrible scourging, the crown-
ing with thorns, Calvary. He looked with merciful love at
those who had wounded his hands and his feet because those
wounds were to be the doors to heaven, even for those who
had made them. And he said, "Father, forgive them, for
they know not what they do" *(Lk 22:34)*.

As if that were not enough, he invented the Eucharist:
a God who makes himself into bread, a little host, in order
to descend onto our lips and into our hearts, to bridge all
distance between himself and us.

Love is exacting, love is absolute. So he instituted the
Sacrament which realizes, between him and us, more than
a union, more than a fusion: the oneness of love. He wants
us to become one with him: *ut unum sint (Jn 17:22)*. He
could only bring about this oneness by changing us into
himself.

Yes, truly, he loved us immensely. He loved us with an
incomprehensible love which surpasses all words on earth. He
loved us to the utmost limit. St. John finds only these words

for it: "He loved them unto the end" *(Jn 13:1)*.

What I have just told you, you know by heart. It is the Gospel, nothing else. You have learned it since your childhood. You have grown up deepening your understanding of these mysteries. But we do not read the Gospel enough in the light of the love of Christ.

Thus, sixteen centuries after the Last Supper and Calvary, the most satanic of all heresies, Jansenism, was able to appear and spread: a heresy which turned a God of love, saying with open arms, "Come to me, all of you, come because you are unworthy, come because you are sinful, come because you need to be saved," into a God whose arms are raised to strike, a demanding God, a vengeful God. Under the pretext of recognizing our unworthiness, Jansenism diabolically led souls away from Jesus.

Thus, no longer willing to endure this heresy, he appeared to St. Margaret Mary at Paray-le-Monial and through her gave his Heart to the world. "Here is the Heart which loved men so much that it spared nothing, to the point of being emptied and consumed, to give them proof of that love."

Before Paray-le-Monial, Jesus could think, "I have given them everything. I have given them my sweat and fatigue on the roads of Palestine; I have given them all my blood on Calvary; I have given them the gift of my beloved Mother; I have given myself in the Eucharist. What more can I do that they may believe in my love? I know, I shall give them my Heart; I shall give them the source of all these follies of my love. But if they do not love me, after giving them the gift of my Heart, when will they love me?"

Meditate on the love of Jesus in his Gospel, on the love of Jesus in his own life, as we have just briefly done. Then meditate on the love of Jesus in your own life.

We have spoken of his love for everyone; let us now talk about his love for you, personally. This is a meditation which

you will not find in books. It is a meditation you will discover in the book of your life.

Why are you here? Why were you born into a Christian
family? Why were you baptized? Why have you learned to
know Jesus, to love him since your earliest childhood? Because he has chosen you and preferred you from all eternity,
to heap these graces upon you. Recall your first prayers,
your confirmation, your first Communion, that first union of
your soul with him, your infidelities, small or great, Jesus
picking you up again, becoming for you so many times the
Good Shepherd, running after his little lamb, carrying it
back in his arms; the absolution you have received so often
in the sacrament of penance, this pouring out of his divine
blood, which purifies you in an instant. Why again do you
have this grace of being chosen to be a part of a Christian
elite, called to make retreats? Because you have been loved
with predilection. There is no other explanation. And if there
are any converts among you, you must unite yourselves
with the thanksgiving of a St. Paul or a St. Augustine.
What confidence he had in you, to give himself in this way.
One could say that you were in some way a need of his
Heart.

Many among you have always been faithful, others perhaps have resisted his calls for a long time, others may
have fallen very low. Who are those Jesus loves best? No
one can know that. At Calvary there was John the beloved,
the marvelously faithful and pure apostle; and there was
Mary Magdalene, the great sinner, the scandalous one who
repented. They were there, both of them, near the Cross as
equals. On the morning of the Resurrection it was to Mary
Magdalene that Jesus appeared first of all, even before
appearing to his apostles, and he sent her to announce the
great news. He made her the apostle of the apostles. What
predilection! *(cf. Jn. 20:17)*.

I shall come back to this, but I should like to ask you
urgently, from now on, that you never let your past sins
be an obstacle between you and Jesus. It is a ruse of the

devil to "keep putting our sins before our eyes in order to make them like a screen between the Savior and us. Think of your past sins for your own humiliation, or to persuade yourself once again of your weakness, of your unworthiness; think of them in order to find happiness in expiation, in order to confirm your firm resolution not to fall again—certainly that is necessary—but especially in order to bless Jesus for having pardoned you, for having purified you, for having cast all your sins to the bottom of the sea. *Projiciet in profundum maris omnia peccata nostra (Mi 7:19).* Do not go looking for them at the bottom of the sea! He has wiped them out, he has forgotten them. His blood has been shed, the flames of his mercy have done their work, they have burned up all of them, consumed them all while renewing you yourselves. Our faults must remain for us a source of humility and repentance, but especially a source of immense thankfulness for the forgiveness we have received, a source of limitless faith in a limitless mercy; a faith, moreover, which (to the extent that it is filled with love), obtains the remission of the punishment we deserve for our sins.

If you have been loved like this, you must love in return, give love for Love. "I have loved you, you must love. I have given you my Heart without reserve, in order to have your heart without reserve; I have put no limit on my love, you must put no limit on yours."

The first commandment you know: "You shall love the Lord your God with your whole heart, with your whole soul and with your whole mind" *(Mt 22:37).* This commandment contains all the others and it is for everyone.

When Jesus founded his Church on Peter, he asked him the same question three times: "Peter, do you love me?" He could have said, "Peter, will you be a man of character, capable of leading your brothers to follow in your path? Will you be a wise man, capable of instructing them and explaining things to them? a model of virtue, as an example to them?" He did not ask a single one of those

questions, but only, "Peter, do you love me?" That is all.
If Peter loved Jesus, the Holy Spirit would be in him and
he would lack nothing he needed to feed the lambs and
the sheep.

"Love therefore is the fulfilling of the law," said St. Paul
(Rom 13:10) and St. Augustine: "Love, and do what you
will."

Listen to St. John of the Cross affirming that "the smallest movement of pure love is worth more to the Church
than all works put together." And little Thérèse, on the
very eve of her death, said to her sister Céline, "I have
said everything. Everything is accomplished. It is love alone
that counts."[6] After her death a deluge of miracles fell
from heaven to make us say, "She was not wrong; it is
love alone that counts."

I made a pilgrimage to Assisi, Paray-le-Monial, Ars,
Lisieux, and in these cities which still, across the centuries,
remain filled with the celestial perfume of the saints who
lived there, I asked myself, "How were Francis, the holy
Curé, Margaret Mary, and Thérèse able to accomplish the
divine mission which was theirs in the Holy Church?" And
the answer came to me for each one, like a refrain, *"Dilexit,*
. . . he loved . . . she loved."

For a well-known cardinal, all dogma was contained in
this word: *"Dilexi te,"* "I have loved you"; all morality
in this other word, *"Diligam te,"* "That I may love you!"

A holy soul said to our Savior, "Why do you come to
earth like this to seek love? You have in heaven your angels
and your saints who love you with an unstained love, while
here below all our righteousness is like a stain to your
eyes." And Jesus answered, "I come to earth to seek love,
to beg for love, because I thirst for love freely given."

Not that the blessed are not free—they are supremely
free, identifying their will with the infinitely free will of
God—for the faculty of sinning is not true freedom, but
rather servitude. But it is of this true freedom that St.

Thomas speaks when he says, "God created man free as one who acts in virtue of free choice, proceeding from his own counsel."

Here on earth love proves itself by free choice. When a man loves, he chooses that which he prefers. Jesus wants to be chosen, to be preferred. That is the great mystery of faith. He hides himself to the point of letting himself be put on the same footing as a creature. Often our nature, wounded by original sin, led astray by concupiscence, deceived by the devil, is tempted to turn away from God. It is then that we can say to him, "Jesus, you whom I have never seen, never heard, who seem sometimes so far away, you who are truly the 'hidden God' *(Is 45:15)*, although the attraction of that which you have denounced is so strong and the forbidden fruit so close, it is you, Jesus, I choose, you I prefer, you I love."

How many times, in the course of the day, in the middle of temptations of various kinds, we have the occasion to give him freely this love which he demands and which must extend to the gift of our freedom itself. Since in heaven our beatitude will consist in being fixed forever in the choice of him which we shall have made, let us use our time in exile to choose him, preferring him to everything else.

What power we have against temptation if we are able to say, "I choose you, Jesus, because I love you." It has been well said that religion is not something, it is Someone. It is the Holy Trinity in us, it is God with us, it is Jesus, chosen and preferred.

"Filioli, my little children, abide in my love" *(Jn 13:30, 15:9)*. In thus asking you for your heart, he gives you life. Love is life, it is the sun, the light, a divine warmth over our whole life. Without this love, you live a shallow life, you vegetate. Externally you do your spiritual exercises, the duties of your state in life, but if your heart is not there, life is not there. Without love, everything is painful, everything is tiring, everything is burdensome. The Cross, taken

up hesitantly, is crushing; taken smilingly, by free will, and with love, it will carry you much more than you carry it. Loves makes time eternal by giving a divine value to everything.

There is an expression which I do not like: "We must carry out the duties of piety," a little like the duty to answer a letter, to pay a visit; or like the duties of servants toward their masters, although what Jesus wants is friendship. He will reward us for our duties done because he is so good, but what an abyss between the two ways of doing things: for duty or for love. Louis Veuillot wrote, "Dry duty is a cold and hard master who does not console anyone and who is terribly boring. Speak to me of loving God, that I may fulfill with joy the duty he assigns to me, and and keep the great joy of love which is sacrifice." In this way, supernaturalize by love the duties of your state in life.

Jesus said, "I have come to cast fire on the earth" *(Lk 12:49)*. Once you yourselves have caught fire, you must spread it to others.

To spread love, we must begin by knowing it, we must begin by believing in it, we must begin by being filled with it, we must begin by living it. Jesus, fill with the fire of your love the "little flock" assembled here to listen to your Word— "to whom it has pleased the Father to give the Kingdom" *(cf. Lk 12:32)*. Give your flock a flame big enough to fill all around it with radiance.

In our time, when hatred is spreading in the world in a terrifying way, we must withstand its assaults, its inundating waves, with a rampart of love.

In the face of Communist Russia and China, of neopaganism, and of creeping materialism, of governments without God, even if they are not his declared enemies, of constitutions in which he is not even mentioned, what can we, the "little flock," do in our weakness? We have all the power of love at our disposal, the omnipotence of Jesus who said, "Have confidence, I have overcome the world" *(Jn 16:33)*.

But the victory depends on our faith in him, on our hope, on our charity.

Oh, how beautiful it is, how encouraging, that the weaker we are, and the more we feel our weakness, the more this power of Jesus, if we are united to him, is ours.

"When I am weak, then am I powerful" cries St. Paul *(2 Cor 12:10).*

I want to put you on guard right now against the danger of sensible love. How often I have heard the objection, "I tell Jesus that I love him, but I don't feel it. It seems to me that I'm not being sincere." Not to doubt that you love him when you feel cold and arid, demands great faith, the forgetting of oneself and a true understanding of sanctity.

The greatest saints passed through the dark night of the soul, painful periods of dryness. Yet in those hours of purification they loved.

Love is not sensible piety. Never forget this distinction. Holiness is a disposition of the soul, of the heart, and above all, of the will, toward God; the senses may play a role, but it is not necessary.

Little Thérèse writes that dryness was her daily bread, but that she was nevertheless the happiest of creatures.[7] She defined sanctity as "a disposition of the heart which makes us humble and small in the arms of God, conscious of our weakness, and confident to the point of audacity in the goodness of our Father."[8]

Love is the uniting of our will to the will of God. It is abandoning ourselves totally into his hands, as a habitual disposition, even if we feel nothing. When Jesus sees this disposition in our hearts, he looks on us as his cherished children. Is not a father very indulgent toward his child? He finds excuses for his failings and he admires the least of his good qualities. Jesus is like this with those who are his children because they sincerely want to be such.

However persistently he repeats to us in the Gospel, "Fear not, it is I," the fear is still there: "If I go to him, what

will he ask of me? What will he require of me? I am afraid,
I wouldn't want to hurt him, to wound him. As for com-
pletely giving myself to him, that is risking too much. . . ."
But it is just this fear that wounds him.

St. Teresa of Avila observes that the Samaritan, the
Canaanite woman, Mary Magdalene were not dead to the
world when they found Jesus.

St. Francis de Sales said, "We must begin with love,
continue with love, and end with love." When a religious
sister had told him, "I wish to acquire love through humility," he replied, "And I wish to acquire humility through
love."

My principal aim, in this retreat, is to give some answers
to your personal problems, those, in short, which preoccupy
you most, sometimes to the point of anguish, because it has
to do with the eternal life of your soul and because on your
sanctity depends the light that will radiate through you upon
your neighbor and the world.

Einstein said, "The present problem is not that of atomic
energy, but that of the human heart." It is a problem which
Jesus alone can resolve. We speak admirably about him,
but we do not speak to him. The first dialogue must be
with him.

Often I ask the question, "Do you think you are a joy
for Jesus?" How many times I have been answered, "I
never thought about that." Or people protest, saying that
to think such a thing would be a lack of humility and would
ignore our wretchedness. I shall speak to you at length
about this in the course of the retreat. Yet is it not a matter of the most elementary logic that a father and his child
should be a joy for one another? "Jesus, you are my joy,
and I too am your joy." Is it not written that "his delight
is to be with the children of men?" *(Prv 8:31)*.

There are persons who are baptized, who are confirmed,
who receive Communion, who are souls in a state of grace,
temples of the Holy Spirit, who pass their whole lives on
earth without ever having experienced this heart to heart

relationship with their Father in heaven, their Creator and Savior, in the happiness which comes from being a joy for one another. Is not the life of grace the beginning of eternal beatitude?

People examine themselves in terms of what is forbidden them and not in terms of what is asked of them. People examine themselves on faults and failings, and not on their intimacy with Jesus. It has been rightly said that sins of omission—of which we so rarely think to accuse ourselves—are more frequent that the others: lack of faith, of hope, and of charity, failure to believe in God's merciful love and to live in it.

I assure you, we are bathed in love and mercy. We each have a Father, a Brother, a Friend, a Spouse of our soul, Center and King of our hearts, Redeemer and Savior, bent down over us, over our weakness and our impotence, like that of little children, with an inexpressible gentleness, watching over us like the apple of his eye, who said, "I will have mercy and not sacrifice, for I have not come to call the just, but sinners" *(Mt 9:13)*, a Jesus haunted by the desire to save us by all means, who has opened heaven under our feet. And we live, too often, like orphans, like abandoned children, as if it were hell which had opened under our feet. We are men of little faith!

Oh, how I would love it if at the end of this conference and even more at the end of this retreat you were able to cry out with the psalmist, "Lord, you have opened my heart and I run in the way of your commandments" *(Ps 118:32)*.

Chapter 2

Humble Confidence

~~~~~~

You must believe in the love of Jesus for you. Love calls for love. How do you give Jesus love for Love? Before all and above all by your confidence in him.

This word, confidence, summarizes the three theological virtues, faith, hope and charity: sovereign virtues which bring all the others in their train. But if these are the highest virtues, then the greatest heroism is demanded of us in order to realize them in the face of the mystery of a "hidden God."

A man must be heroic to live always in faith, hope, and love. Why? Because, as a result of original sin no one can be certain with the certainty of faith that he is saved,[1] but only with a moral certainty based upon fidelity to grace, and because as sinners we are constantly tempted by doubt and anxiety.

It was in order to resolve this conflict between our desires and our powerlessness that he came to earth and took our infirmities upon himself *(Mt 8:17)*.

Little Thérèse understood that it is our state of misery which attracts his mercy.

Before her, St. Paul wrote, "Gladly therefore will I glory in my infirmities, that the power of Christ may dwell in me" *(2 Cor 12:9)*.

"I can do all things in him who strengthens me" *(Phil 4:13)*. How profound is the theology of St. Paul! He glories in his infirmities, he rejoices in being weak because Jesus is there.

For it is this confidence, and nothing but confidence, which will open the arms of Jesus to you so that he will bear you up. It is confidence which will be for you the golden key to his Heart.

In her desire to be holy, and comparing herself to the saints, St. Thérèse said that there was, between them and herself, the same difference as between a mountain whose summit is lost in the heavens and an obscure grain of sand, trampled under the feet of passers-by. Rather than becoming discouraged, she thought, "The good God would not inspire unattainable desires; I can, then, in spite of my littleness, aspire to sanctity. For me to become greater is impossible; I must put up with myself just as I am with all my imperfections. But I wish to find the way to go to heaven by a very straight, short, completely new little way. We are in a century of inventions: now one does not even have to take the trouble to climb the steps of a stairway; in the homes of the rich an elevator replaces them nicely. I too would like to find an elevator to lift me up to Jesus, for I am too little to climb the rough stairway of perfection. So I have looked in the books of the saints for a sign of the elevator I long for, and I have read these words proceeding from the mouth of eternal Wisdom: 'He that is a little one, let him turn to me' *(Prv 9:16)*. So I came, knowing that I had found what I was seeking, and wanting to know, O my God, what you would do with the little one who would answer your call, and this is what I found:

'As one whom the mother caresses, so will I comfort you. You shall be carried at the breasts and upon the knees they shall caress you' *(Is 66:12-13)*. Never have more tender words come to make my soul rejoice. The elevator which must raise me to the heavens is your arms, O Jesus! For that I do not need to grow; on the contrary, I must necessarily remain small, become smaller and smaller. O my God, you have surpassed what I expected and I want to sing your mercies."[2]

All the theology of little Thérèse, which echoes that of St. Paul, is summarized and put at our disposal in these lines, on which we could meditate endlessly without exhausting their richness.

What I cannot do myself Jesus will do. He will take me and lift me up to the summit of the mountain of perfection, to the summit of the mountain of love.

It is true that instinctively we seek to climb the rough stairway of perfection instead of taking the gentle elevator of the arms of Jesus. This is because we have been told so often of our miseries. We have been told, and rightly, that we are miserable; and then, we have been told about Jesus, that he is good, yes, but not enough that he is wondrously good, infinitely good, infinite charity. No one has told us at the same time that he is Savior before he is Judge and that, in the Heart of God, "justice and peace have embraced" *(Ps 84:11)*.

We have been trained in the habit of looking at our dark side, our ugliness, and not at the purifying Sun, Light of Light, which he is, who changes the dust that we are into pure gold. We think about examining ourselves, yet we do not think, before the examination, during the examination, and after the examination, to plunge ourselves, with all our miseries, into the consuming and transforming furnace of his Heart, which is open to us through a single humble act of confidence.

I am not telling you, "You believe too much in your own wretchedness." We are much more wretched than we ever realize. But I am telling you, "You do not believe enough in merciful Love."

We must have confidence, not in spite of our miseries, but because of them, since it is misery which attracts mercy.

Oh, this word, mercy—*misericordia*—*"miseris cor dare,"*[3] a Heart which gives itself to the miserable, a Heart which nourishes itself on miseries by consuming them. Meditate on this word.

St. Thomas says that "to have mercy belongs to the nature of God, and it is in this that his omnipotence manifests itself in the highest degree."[4]

Little Thérèse perceived this when she wrote these lines

which complete and crown her manuscript: "Yes, I sense
that even if I had on my conscience all the sins which can
be committed, I would go, my heart broken, to repent and
throw myself into the arms of Jesus, for I know how much
he cherishes the prodigal child who returns to him. It is not
because the dear Lord in his provident mercy has preserved
my soul from mortal sin that I am lifted up to him by confidence and love."[5]

Again, shortly before her death, speaking to Mother
Agnes, she said, "You may truly say that if I had committed all possible crimes, I would still have the same confidence, I would feel that this multitude of offenses would be
like a drop of water thrown into a flaming furnace."[6] All
possible crimes, a multitude of offenses, a drop of water in
an immense furnace: that is the proportion.

And this affirmation is so logical it is irrefutable.

When I have preached this doctrine of confidence in the
midst of our misery, taking my support from little Thérèse,
I have often, very often, met with this objection: "Yes,
she was marvelously confident, but she could say that 'from
the age of three years she had never refused God anything.'[7] If I, too, could claim never to have refused Jesus
anything since my childhood, it would be easy for me to be
confident as she was."

Yes, people have made this objection, and I have always
understood why it was made. But she foresaw it and answers it in the last sentence of her great letter to Sister
Marie of the Sacred Heart, a fundamental monument of her
doctrine. It is like a will: "Oh, Jesus, how much I could say
to all little souls about how ineffable your condescension is.
. . . I feel that if (though this would be impossible) you
were to find a soul more weak and little than mine, you
would be pleased to shower upon it even greater favors, if
it abandoned itself to you, with complete confidence in your
infinite mercy."[8]

I imagine very clearly what took place in her spirit and
in her heart. She, who so wished to attract little souls to

follow her, thought how they would be tempted to discouragement in seeing how faithful she had been, so she declares that, if there were a soul more miserable than hers, it would receive even more favors, as long as it abandoned itself in complete confidence to infinite mercy. This is true, since merciful Love is for the miserable.

I want to tell you something in confidence. These words had a decisive influence on the orientation of my own interior life.

One day, seeing that I fulfilled perfectly the first condition of the program, to be weaker than St. Thérèse, I decided to apply myself with my whole soul to fulfilling the second: to abandon myself in complete confidence.

She knew the weight of the words she used. She asks self-abandonment, and I shall show you that abandonment rightly understood is the greatest of all renunciations. And she asks more than immense confidence, more than confidence to the point of foolishness; she asks complete confidence—that is to say, a confidence as great as our weakness, as great as our misery.

Of course, when we see ourselves to be so unworthy, so faint-hearted, falling every moment, how could we not be tempted against confidence? The question occurs, "Is the love of Jesus, his merciful love, really so great? Is it as great as that?" His merciful love is without limits, his mercy is infinite.

That is why you can and you must live this doctrine which opens the Kingdom of Heaven to the most miserable and the road of sanctity to the poorest. I insist so emphatically upon this point because I know that the consideration of our miseries is an objection which returns constantly in our daily struggle to advance in perfection.

And more than St. Paul, more than little Thérèse, it is the Gospel which teaches us this doctrine of salvation. It is the Gospel where we see that what Jesus asks of us, before and above all, is humility and confidence.

Look at the prodigal son. He leaves his father's house.

He displays frightful ingratitude toward his father who is so good; he demands his part of the inheritance to go carousing, far away. Soon, he finds himself stripped of everything and is forced to reflect. In the depths of his abjection, he has the grace to recall the goodness of his father. "I shall rise up and go to my father." That is confidence.

But, humbly, he recognizes himself to be a sinner. "I shall say to him, Father, I have sinned against heaven and before you; I am not worthy to be called your son. Make me as one of your hired servants" *(Lk 15:18)*.

You know how the father received him, not as a servant, but as a beloved son. Seeing him coming from afar, he runs to meet him; seized with compassion, he throws himself on his neck, presses him to his heart, and embracing him, he tells his servants: "Bring forth quickly the first robe and put it on him and put a ring on his hand and shoes on his feet: and bring hither the fatted calf and kill it and let us eat and make merry." And there was dancing and music. These eloquent details with which the story ends show us a father exulting in his happiness. And why? He tells us why, and repeats it to the jealous older brother: "This my son was dead and has come to life again; was lost and has been found."

Oh, this desire, this need of the Father of Mercies to retrieve his lost child and give him life! That is the Heart of God!

Remember that each time you pick yourself up after a fall, the feast of the prodigal son is renewed. Your Father in heaven clothes you again in his most beautiful cloak, puts a ring on your finger, and tells you to dance with joy. In a living faith, you will not approach the confessional with dragging feet, but as if you were going to a feast, even if you have to make a great effort each time to humble yourself and to conquer the monotony of the routine.

After the absolution, you should dance like the prodigal son did at the request and for the joy of his father. We do not dance enough in the spiritual life.

This marvelous parable gives us a fundamental lesson about education. Parents, educators, give the children confided to your care an understanding of this divine mercy by believing in it and practicing it yourselves. It is this faith which will prevent them from falling again and, if they fall, they will rise again, they will come back because you will have acquainted them with the gentleness of God. They will say, "I know how good God is. I know how to abide in his mercy. From the depths of my sin, I shall rise up and go to my father."

They are happy parents who have shown this way to their children, without weakness or compromise, but with a goodness so like that of God that, in their worst difficulties, they can say humbly with tremendous confidence, "I shall rise up and go to my father, I shall rise up and go to my mother; and through them, I shall go to my Father in heaven." How many young people have lost the Faith, not from having fallen, but from not having been helped, with love, to pick themselves up again as many times as was necessary.

The good thief also teaches us humility and confidence. A whole life of crimes, a whole life of sin: a few minutes before dying, one word of humility and confidence, and he is saved.

In the same way as the prodigal son recognized his guilt, the good thief, speaking to his companion, cries, "For us, this is justice; we have received what we deserve." Then he looks deep into the eyes of Jesus, and reads there who he is: the gentle Savior.

"Lord, remember me when you shall come into your kingdom" *(Lk 23:40)*.

And the ineffable answer is, "Amen, I say to you, this day you shall be with me in Paradise." For you, no hell, not a second of purgatory. The confident look you gave me, this meeting of our eyes, in my mercy and in your faith, has purified you in an instant and rendered us inseparable. Now you are completely pure, and already in heaven.

A whole life of sin, one humble and confident look toward

the Crucified, and there was the first canonized saint, and canonized by Jesus himself! A thief who stole heaven!

When you see how miserable you are after an act of infidelity, a failure which has humiliated you, if you look toward Jesus, with the look of the good thief, do you not believe that you will be purified in a moment, in a second, as he was, and more than he, you who make retreats in order to love him better? You will, on the condition that you have the humility of the good thief and his confidence and desire for heaven.

Jesus needs nothing but your humility and your confidence to work marvels of purification and sanctification in you. And your confidence will be in proportion to your humility because it is to the extent that we realize our need of Jesus that we have recourse to him, and we sense this need to the extent that we justly realize our unworthiness.

Think of the woman of Canaan: she is a pagan, a foreigner. She asks Jesus to cure her daughter who is possessed by a demon. Jesus lets her see that since he has come for the lost sheep of Israel, he has nothing to do with her. Humbly she accepts this, which is the truth, but confidently she insists, "Lord, come to my aid." And Jesus shows himself to be apparently even harder. Often he acts in this way with souls to whom he wishes to grant a high place in his love, in order to test their faith. He answers her, "The bread of the children is not to be thrown to the dogs." The Canaanite woman then finds, in her humble confidence, this exquisitely appropriate response: "That is true, Lord, but even the dogs eat the crumbs which fall from their master's table." She asks no more than a crumb at the banquet of merciful Love! Jesus is conquered.

"Oh woman, great is your faith, be it done to you as you will." *Fiat tibi sicut vis (Mt 15:28).*

"You have stolen my Heart, you have stolen my will from me by your faith filled with love; I can refuse you nothing."

Is it too much to say, after that, that confident souls steal God's omnipotence?

You who are not foreigners, you who are not dogs under the table, but the children of the house by your baptism, you can, you must go to Jesus with even more assurance than the Canaanite woman, recognizing that you merit nothing, but expecting everything from a completely gratuitous and infinite mercy.

Recall the centurion: it is always the same thing—humility and confidence. "Lord I am not worthy, but speak only a word and my servant shall be healed." And he explains: "I have under me soldiers. And I say to one, 'Go,' and he goes, and to another, 'Come,' and he comes, and to my servant, 'Do this,' and he does it" *(Mt 8:8)*.

Jesus replies in admiration of such logic, "Amen I say to you, I have not found so great faith in Israel. . . . As you have believed, be it done to you."

In the manner of the centurion, you also must say, "I am not worthy to receive you, I merit nothing, I am an abyss of weakness and cowardice; I make resolutions and do not keep them; I fall over and over again, but Jesus, say only one word and my soul shall be healed."

Jesus was so delighted by the centurion's words that he willed them to be fixed in the liturgy of the Mass, to be forever the most perfect preparation for Communion.

I can imagine the centurion in heaven, enjoying the unspeakable glory and beatitude of hearing these words, which came from his heart, repeated at the moment when Jesus is received in the Host by all priests and all communicants, in all the Masses which are celebrated in the entire world until the end of time. What a heaven for him! What glory! Why? Because he recognized his own unworthiness, and he believed.

When Jesus tests your faith, give him, like the Canaanite woman and the centurion, these responses that eternal Wisdom inspires in the little ones *(cf. Prv 1:4)*, and he will be filled with admiration *(cf. Mt 8:10)* for you, too, and will shower his graces upon you.

What does he lament most when he is with his apostles? Their lack of confidence. "Men of little faith!" This is the

main reproach he makes to them. He does not say to them,
"Men of no character, men without energy, without dis-
cipline." No, he says, "Men of little faith!"

Jesus was crossing the lake of Tiberias in a boat with his
disciples. He was asleep in the stern. A great windstorm
blew up and the waves poured into the boat so that it was
already filled. Seized with anguish the disciples awakened
Jesus: "Lord, save us, we are perishing!" And rising up, he
reprimands the wind and says to the sea, "Peace! Be still!"
"And the wind abated and there was a great calm." Then,
turning to his apostles, he asks, "Where is your faith?" *(Mk
4:40).* I can hear Jesus scolding them with gentleness, but
with pain, too: "Why is this? I was in the boat with you—I
slept, but I was there—and you were afraid, you were terri-
fied. You doubted either my omnipotence or my love. Do you
not know after all who I am, and do you not know after all
with what tenderness my Heart watches over you continually?" It is truly such doubt that pains and offends him
most.

But you see, we have lost so completely the notion of the
entire confidence that he expects of us, that we sometimes
make a prayer of the words for which he reproached his
apostles: "Lord, save us, we are perishing!"

This is not how we should pray, but rather, "With you,
Jesus, I cannot perish; you are always in the boat with me;
what have I to fear? You may sleep; I shall not awaken you.
My poor nature will tremble, oh yes! But with all my will I
shall remain in peace in the midst of the storm, confident in
you."

In hours of anguish, think of the Divine Master calming
the violent storm with one word. This will be a tremendous
source of comfort for you as you wait—peacefully—for him
to waken.

The great tempest is what our sins stir up in our souls. It
is there that Jesus must arise in order that "a great calm
may descend."

Listen to what little Thérèse has to say in the fable about

the weak little bird who, not having wings strong enough to soar in the heights, at least has eyes and a heart to gaze at the Sun of Love: "With bold abandonment, he remains gazing at his Divine Sun. Nothing can frighten him, neither wind nor rain; and if dark clouds come to hide the Star of Love, the weak little bird will not move away, for he knows that on the other side of the clouds his Sun continues always to shine."[9]

"I am not always faithful, but I never get discouraged. I abandon myself into the arms of Jesus and there I find again all that I have lost and much more besides."[10]

"Since he has granted it to me to understand the Love of the Heart of Jesus, I confess that he has chased all fear out of my heart. The memory of my faults humiliates me, leads me never to rely on my own strength which is nothing but weakness; but even more this memory speaks to me of mercy and love. When we throw our faults, with a completely filial confidence, into the devouring furnace of Love, how could they not be totally consumed?"[11]

Here we reach an essential point in the "little way." It is that a soul that is disposed to please Jesus in everything, that has committed everything to him in freely committing its will—and these souls are more numerous than one might think—a soul that has made an oblation as a victim to merciful Love (I shall return to this), an act which the weakest souls are called to make because they are "more fitted to the operations of consuming and transforming Love,"[12] such a soul, in its thirst for purity, can remember that it is continually purified in the fire of Love.

"Ah, since this happy day [of my offering] it seems to me," cries little Thérèse, "that each moment this merciful love renews me, purifies my soul and leaves on it no trace of sin."[13]

She sees herself to be pure, not by her own efforts—no one is confirmed in grace—but because she has been purified and renewed and regenerated in the fire of mercy to which she has delivered herself.

Two months before her death, when someone said to her, "You are a saint," she answered, pointing to the tops of the trees in the garden, golden in the setting sun, "My soul appears to you to be all brilliant and golden because it is exposed to the rays of Love. If the Divine Sun stopped sending me his fire, I would immediately become dark and full of shadows."[14]

Thus the soul which suffers to see itself tarnished by its faults and failings, and which exposes itself to the rays of the divine, transforming Sun, can say to Jesus, "Jesus, I come to you completely beautiful, beautiful like the Sun which you are, pure with your own purity, beautiful with your own beauty, rich with your own treasures." That is the *copiosa redemptio (Ps 127:7).*

See what a life of love is established between Jesus and us in such a union. I need to have constant recourse to him, but he is always there, and my need for him is always satisfied. Jesus purifies us each moment, but we must desire it with an immense desire and believe in it.

To the sick who asked him to cure them on the roads of Palestine, he posed only one question: "Do you believe that I can heal you?" "Yes , Lord!" "Be it done unto you as you have believed" *(Mt 9:28,29).* He says to you now, "Do you believe that I can purify you in a moment and wipe from your soul every trace of sin?" "Yes, Lord, I believe." "Then it is done," replies the Lord, "because you believe, because you do not doubt it, because you know enough to cling to my infinite mercy, because you remember how I treated the prodigal son, the good thief, the woman of Canaan, when they vanquished me by their humility and confidence."

St. Margaret Mary heard Jesus say to her, "Do you believe that I can do it? If you believe it, you will see the power of my Heart in the magnificence of my love."

Moral misery is a sickness much greater than a disease. I desire to be purified much more than the blind man desired to see or the paralytic to walk. We must have this sincere desire—but you do have it; if you did not you would not be here.

We touch here upon the very basis of the interior life, the basis of the Redemption, the basis of the Gospel. Live this faith, this hope, and this love. Live the theological virtues, so named because they lead us to God and unite us to him. Live this humble confidence and "all the rest will be added unto you" *(Mt 6:33)*. It is this which intimately unites the soul to Jesus, which brings us heart to Heart with him, which grafts the branch again into the vine which he is.

"If anyone thirst,"—and especially if he thirst for purity and love—"let him come to me; let him drink who believes in me *(Jn 7, 37-38)*.

We know that souls who thirst in this way constantly return with fervor to the sacrament of penance, a marvelous source of humility, and a means to know their faults better and to repent of them in the supernatural joy of confessing them; in spite of natural repugnance, an occasion to renew wholeheartedly the firm purpose of amendment and especially an occasion to plunge themselves once more, like the prodigal son, into the furnace of mercy. Even if they think that their Communions, their use of the sacramentals, their confident acts of love have already purified them, they will go faithfully to receive, along with the absolution, a purification which is most special because it is sacramental, a new effusion upon them of the blood of Jesus, their only hope, without forgetting that this recourse is necessary only for serious sins.

I imagine you are like me. I need to be happy, I need to live on love, I need to be festive, I need to sing, and for all that, to which my being aspires, I need to know that I am forgiven.

Psychiatrists attribute most of the neuroses and mental disequilibrium so common today to the suffering caused by feelings of guilt. The remedy proposed by unbelievers is to suppress the notion of sin, to remove from man the sense of sin. This is obviously a radical remedy. But it does not succeed. The conscience is still there. They may succeed in partially and temporarily stifling it, but they cannot kill it, any more than they can kill God.

No, the remedy is the peace which Jesus gives us in the certainty that we are forgiven because we are loved.

Saint John declares, "If we say that we have no sin, we deceive ourselves, and the truth is not in us. If we confess our sins, he is faithful and just, to forgive us our sins, and to cleanse us from all iniquity" *(1 Jn 1:8-9)*.

Our love for God is a love of friendship, a love received and given. Since, in friendship, a certain equality is necessary between the two friends, God has made himself man, has brought himself down to our level, has made himself like us; and correspondingly, he has raised us up to himself by sanctifying grace.

Thus we can realize with him the life of friendship of which St. Thomas speaks with admirable insight: "In the love proper to friendship, he who loves is in his friend by the fact that he makes his own the fortunes and even the misfortunes of his friend. Also it is proper to friends to will the same things." What constitutes friendship, then, is mutual confidence in unity of will.

Jesus has a Heart like ours. He took it in order to be able to love us as we would love him. That is why a sin of defiance offends and hurts him more than a hundred sins of weakness.

I have often noticed that to reward an act of confidence, Jesus gives us the occasion to make an even greater act of confidence. Recall the scene on the lake. The apostles are in the boat which is being battered about by waves, for the wind is rough. At the fourth watch of the night, Jesus comes toward them walking on the sea. The disciples mistake him for a ghost and cry out in fear. Immediately Jesus says, "Have confidence, it is I, be not afraid." Peter says, "Lord, if it is you, command me to come to you on the water." "Come," answers Jesus. Peter rushes out onto the water, but seeing the violence of the wind, he is afraid and as he starts to sink, he cries, "Lord, save me!" Then Jesus extends his hand, takes hold of him, and says, "Man of little faith, why did you doubt?"

Peter had made a beautiful act of confidence by jumping out onto the sea. To reward him, Jesus gave him a chance to make an even greater act of confidence by permitting him to sink into the water. Peter made the first act of confidence but, alas, not the second!

Martha and Mary demonstrated their confidence in Jesus in an exquisite fashion at the bedside of the dying Lazarus by sending him a message which was a prayer of marvelous delicacy and proved how they knew his Heart, his compassion, his friendship for Lazarus: "Lord, behold, he whom you love is sick!" How touched Jesus must have been by such a prayer! To reward Martha and Mary for the tenderness of their confidence, he permitted Lazarus to die, giving them the chance to demonstrate a confidence a thousand times greater by an act of faith in his omnipotence. Jesus brought Lazarus back to life, but before he did so, he required, as always, an act of faith.

Jesus reminds Martha who he is: "I am the Resurrection and the Life. He who believes in me, although he be dead, shall live. . . . Do you believe this?" That is the great question, the condition for the miracle. "Do you believe that I can do it? Do you believe that I am going to do it, that I am going to bring your brother back to life?" Martha makes the act of faith: "Yes, Lord, . . . I believe that you are the Christ, the Son of the living God." She has already said to him, "I know that whatsoever you will ask of God, God will give it to you."

This is what Jesus is like with those who love him. He does not grant the first prayer; he permits a greater trial. And we become distressed: "I have prayed and I have not been heard. All is lost; all is finished. God does not listen to me. He does not love me." Because God loves you, he wants to see how far you will push your confidence. He wants to be able to say to you, as he did to the Canaanite woman, "How great is your faith!"

Do not be like Peter sinking in the waves, but rather like Martha and Mary before the tomb of Lazarus, with confidence unto death. Believe, believe in the divine omnipotence! Believe in Love! "Lord, increase my faith!"

The highest and most complete proof of love is to surrender ourselves completely, giving all our confidence to him whom we love.

Be with Jesus as a friend with his friend, very loving and very beloved. Take your weaknesses and faults to him, as you take him your acts of generosity. The acts of generosity are for the Judge who is so good; the weaknesses and the faults are for the Savior. And everything is for the Friend.

"I will not now call you servants . . . but I have called you friends" *(Jn 15:15).*

Confidence, confidence without limits, full, filial, total, all-inclusive: that is what I want you to take away from this retreat. It is this confidence which works all miracles.

Souls are brought back to life by receiving this secret of heaven. When they have understood, they take wing, they soar, generosity becomes a need for them, and this happens in a spirit of simplicity which removes all danger of presumption and pride.

It is of course necessary to admit that we are all abysses of wretchedness, of sin, since the original sin of Adam. Yet even so, Jesus wants us to be happy. He wills "that (our) joy may be full" *(Jn 16:24).* Peace, his peace, is the happiness which prevails over the suffering of seeing ourselves so full of sin. Jesus will give us this peace in proportion to our confidence in him, to the extent that we do not doubt that it is he who saves us, he who purifies us, he who makes us beautiful, he who says to us, "This very day you shall be with me in paradise." "Begin your paradise with me right now because you have understood that I am the Savior and that I came to earth to give men the peace of my Heart, the heaven of my Heart here below."

"Peace to men of good will" *(Lk 2:14)*. "Peace I leave with you, my peace I give unto you" *(Jn 14:27)*.

It is such happiness for Jesus to see a soul profit fully from his Redemption and the price of his blood, for after all, if he came down from heaven, if he performed all these "foolish" acts of love, the Incarnation, Calvary, and the Eucharist, why was it? In order to make us happy by giving us a hundredfold here below, and the possession of eternal life *(Mt 19:29)*. "Behold your king comes to you, meek, and sitting upon an ass" *(Mt 21:5)*.

Is that an unattainable spirituality? It is nothing but the Gospel, and the Gospel is for everyone.

Let us conclude with the admirable exhortation of St. Paul to the Philippians where we find the joy, the charity, the confidence, the prayer, the thanksgiving, the marvelous peace which surpasses all understanding in Christ Jesus.

"Rejoice in the Lord always, again I say, rejoice. Let your modesty be known to all men. The Lord is nigh. Be nothing solicitous; but in everything, by prayer and supplication, with thanksgiving, let your petitions be made known to God. And the peace of God, which surpasses all understanding, keep your hearts and minds in Christ Jesus" *(Phil 4:4.)*.

Chapter 3

Unshakeable Confidence

〰〰〰〰〰〰〰〰〰〰〰〰〰〰〰〰〰〰〰〰〰〰〰〰〰〰

St. Paul wrote to Timothy,

"I give him thanks who has strengthened me, even to Christ Jesus our Lord, for that he has counted me faithful, putting me in the ministry, who before was counted a blasphemer and a persecutor and contumelious. But I obtained the mercy of God because I did it ignorantly, in unbelief. Now the grace of our Lord has abounded exceedingly with faith and love, which is in Christ Jesus.

"A faithful saying, and worthy of all acceptation that Christ Jesus came into this world to save sinners, of whom I am the chief. But for this cause have I obtained mercy: that in me first Christ Jesus may show forth all patience, for the information of them who shall believe in him unto life everlasting. Now to the King of Ages immortal, invisible the only God, be honor and glory for ever and ever. Amen" *(1 Tim 1:12-17)*.

Marvelous St. Paul, vessel of election! How he knew the mercy and love of the Beloved! He was showered with favors to serve as an example for us in the way of confidence without limit in the divine mercy. You see we have a good master!

"As for me," declared Blessed Claude de la Colombière, "I glorify you in making known how good you are toward sinners, and that your mercy prevails over all malice, that nothing can destroy it, that no matter how many times, or how shamefully we fall, or how criminally, a sinner need not be driven to despair of your pardon. . . . It is in vain that your enemy and mine sets new traps for me every day. He will make me lose everything else before the hope that I have in your mercy."

And here are expressions of a little known aspect of St.

John Vianney, the holy Curé of Ars, speaking of mercy:
"God's greatest pleasure is to pardon us."

"The good Lord is more eager to pardon a repentant sinner than a mother to rescue her child from the fire."

"In the sacrament of penance, he gives us an infinite share of his mercy."

"Our faults are grains of sand beside the great mountain of the mercies of God."

"God, at the moment of absolution, throws our sins over his shoulder. He forgets them, he annihilates them; they shall never reappear."[1]

See how the saints follow their thought to its final conclusion. The Curé of Ars: "Our sins, grains of sand beside the great mountain of the mercies of God." St. Thérèse of the Child Jesus: "All possible crimes, a drop of water thrown into a blazing furnace."

It has been said that the Curé of Ars copied parts of his sermons from various authors. But the addition of one sentence bursting from his heart, a small rewording of someone else's work, can throw a completely new light onto the theme and give it an unexpected fire, coming from the Holy Spirit. It is the gift of saints who are enlightened, inspired by the Spirit of God, to put their whole souls into what they say. "I throw my soul into their souls," said the holy Curé.

One reproach sometimes made to this spirituality of confident love is that it would entail the danger of presumption and of letting oneself go. You shall see, when I talk to you about abandonment and obedience, how abandonment and obedience do away with this danger. I think, on the contrary, that there is a double danger in the method which diminishes the role of confidence and stresses the role of personal effort, subjected to numerous self-examinations. If we are successful, there is the danger of pride, of attributing to ourselves what is in reality the work of grace; on the other hand, if we see no signs of progress, nine times out of ten, we fall into wretched, sterile discouragement.

Besides, if we live this way, united to Jesus by theological virtues, he himself guards our fidelity and our generosity.

Cardinal Bourne said, "Saint Thérèse of the Child Jesus left mathematics out of the spiritual life and gave the Holy Spirit the role often usurped by directors of conscience."

But in order to live this sound doctrine to the fullest, we must be very convinced. It is not easy to reascend the mountain down which we have been made to slide by Jansenism, which has to some extent affected us all.

Let me tell you something strange: even the most beautiful souls, who burn to be in the Heart of Jesus, do not want to believe that confidence is the key which will open the door for them, because this door is a wound made by love. They look for other ways, as if this way were too beautiful to be reliable. How many times people have said to me, "It is too beautiful to be true." And I answer, "Jesus bought at a dear enough price, at the price of all his blood, the right to bring to earth something 'too beautiful'."

So what then? He calls me just as I am? I can go to him with all my miseries, all my weaknesses? He will repair what I have done badly? He will supply for all my indigence? Yes, provided that you go to him, that you count on him, that you expect everything of him, that you say with St. Paul, *Omnia possum (Phil 4:13):* I can do all things in Him who is my only strength and my only virtue.

A beautiful prayer to pour forth from your heart throughout the day is, "Jesus, repair what I have done badly, supply for what I have left undone."

Or an even more beautiful way to pray is: "Jesus, I know that you make reparation in me, that you supply for me, I know that you will draw the good from the bad that I do, and even, as St. Augustine said, a greater good than if there had been no evil in it." Is this not worthy of adoration? I have a Jesus who does all that in me and for me!

And I am very sure—oh, yes indeed!—that he will never say to me, "You hoped too much of me." I cannot imagine

Jesus saying that.

Notice the nuance I put in this manner of praying. It is good to say, "Jesus, make reparation, supply for me." It is better to say, "Jesus, I know, I am sure that you will do it. I unite myself to that which you bring about in me continually. I unite myself with the marvels you accomplish in my soul without my perceiving it. You hide them from me wisely, to keep me in my littleness, in a fitting mistrust of myself, and to preserve for me all the merit of faith, but I do not doubt it."

Did not Jesus say, "All things, whatsoever you ask when you pray, believe that you have already received them, and they shall come unto you"? *(Mk 11:24)*.

You see how far he wants us to push our confidence: "Believe that you have already received it."

Why are the passages from St. Matthew and St. Luke always cited: "Ask and you shall receive" *(Mt 7:7, Lk 11:9)*, and so rarely this text from St. Mark, so much stronger, so much more revealing of the power of faith, and more in conformity with the divine munificence?

What is more, we must live a presently existing love. Too often, we make our life of love with God in us something to be realized in the future, some day when we shall have made sufficient progress for that. The word "sufficient" makes me smile because, after all, how could we ever establish this sufficiency?

Right away, in the present moment, I say to Jesus that I know that he loves me and that I love him. His arms, his Heart are always open and I can take refuge there this instant, since my wretchedness, far from being an obstacle, is a springboard to propel me there.

What would a husband think who, when asking his wife "Do you love me?" received the response, "I have a great desire to love you, I shall work toward it, I hope one day to achieve it by dint of my efforts and generosity and sacrifice." You are right to smile. But is this not the spiritual disposition many excellent souls adopt toward Jesus?

Make rather the admirable response of St. Peter: "Lord, you know all things, you know that I love you" *(Jn 21:17).* "In spite of appearances, in spite of my coldness and my unworthiness, you know well that I love you. You know it better than I and I do not want to wait until tomorrow to tell you, because loves does not wait."

Convinced of that, never get discouraged. When we see ourselves to be so weak, so impotent, always falling into the same sins, we are tempted to say to ourselves, "Can it be possible that Jesus does not grow weary of this?"

We have all had this temptation at one time or another. "I have promised him so much, I have made so many resolutions, and I always fall again; it is impossible that he does not get tired of it." It is a kind of blasphemy to say that, because it is to limit a mercy which has no limit. It is to doubt the patience, the indulgence, the untiring clemency of Jesus. It is not he who grows weary of us, it is we who grow weary of looking at our ugliness.

During the apparitions of Our Lady at Pontmain the children spelled out, letter by letter, the words they saw being written in the sky, under the feet of the Blessed Virgin. At the word, "allows," *(se laisse)* the adults who saw nothing said to them, "You must be wrong; it must be, "My son is weary," *(se lasse)* and not "My son allows . . ." But instead of "My son has had enough" it was—oh, divine tenderness—"My son allows himself to be moved."

Why do we have this basic tendency, this first impulse to think that Jesus is dissatisfied? Oh, how I would like to help you do away with this atmosphere of distrust, and put you forever into an atmosphere of friendship with your friend Jesus, omnipotent Savior, come for the lost children that we are—lost, but found again like the prodigal son—an atmosphere of hope, a family atmosphere in the mutual confidence of Father and child, which will give you a taste on earth of a happiness which is already heavenly.

Is not the life of glory begun already in the life of grace? Did not St. Paul say, "But our conversation is in heaven"

(Phil 3:20)? and St. John, "Perfect charity casts out fear."
(1 Jn 4:18)?

St. Francis de Sales remarked that the soul which is
preoccupied with fear isolates itself in its weakness. That
is true, and there is nothing sadder.

It is clear that we must examine ourselves in order to
know and readily recognize our profound wretchedness in
all its forms, to suffer bitterly from our sins, but never to
give in to them, never to acknowledge ourselves vanquished,
never to capitulate, to detest ever more what is not good,
what should not be, what is forbidden. Yes, this is clear.
Besides, the more we love Jesus, and the more we draw
near to him, the more we reject whatever does not belong
to him, whatever he condemns.

Moreover, it is he, growing in us and occupying a greater
and greater place in us, who will cause us to detest evil
and sin.

Here is the problem: how can we detest our wretchedness
more each day and at the same time love it? We do not
love our wretchedness itself, we love the consequences of
it—that is to say, we make use of it to immerse ourselves
in humility, then to redouble our confidence and plunge ourselves into the ocean of mercy. Those things go together
very well, very well indeed.

Therefore, never be discouraged by your faults. Begin by
not being astonished at them. A little child who does not
know how to walk is not astonished at stumbling and falling with each step he takes.

Seeing her evil nature and what it produced, St. Teresa
of Avila cried, "There indeed is the kind of thing that grows
in my garden!"

Temptation, humiliating as it is, is an occasion for victory.

"And because you were acceptable to God, it was necessary that temptation should prove you" *(Tb 12:13),* said the
Angel to Tobias.

Even a fall strengthens us if we repent it, since Jesus brings good out of evil. Go to him as to a fountain of living water, as many times as necessary, picking yourself up each time more humble and each time more overflowing with confident love. If you make each sin an occasion for you to kiss the wound of his Heart with repentance and confidence, each sin will become a rung in the ladder by which you ascend in love. From misery to misery we go from mercy to mercy.

I have already told how little Thérèse understood, lived, and expressed this doctrine, but I come back to her again, for truly, she is the one who taught it.

She took pleasure in recounting her infidelities in detail to Jesus, thinking, in her bold abandonment, to attract more fully, to gain a greater hold on the love of him who did not come to call the just, but sinners.[2]

She wrote to her sister Céline: "We would like to suffer generously, grandly, Céline, but what an illusion! We would like never to fall! What does it matter, my Jesus, if I fall every moment? It shows me my weakness and it is a great gain for me. It shows you what I am capable of and then you will be more tempted to carry me in your arms. If you do not do so, it will be because it pleases you to see me on the ground."[3] "Céline, if you are willing to endure in peace the trial of not pleasing yourself, you will provide a sweet refuge to the Divine Master. It is true that you will suffer, since you will thus be dispossessed, but do not fear: the poorer you are, the more Jesus will love you."[4]

After having shown impatience toward one of her sisters, she wrote to Mother Agnes, "I am much more happy to have been imperfect than if, upheld by grace, I had been a model of sweetness. It does me so much good to see that Jesus is always just as gentle, just as tender with me. Why does he not scold me?"[5]

She recognized very quickly that, the more one advances on the way of perfection, the further one believes oneself from the goal. She was also resigned to see herself always imperfect and to find her joy in this.[6] And she cried, "How happy I am to see myself imperfect and having so great a need of receiving the mercy of God at the moment of death!"[7] Even in the very arms of death!

"Instead of rejoicing in my dryness, I ought to attribute it to my lack of fervor and fidelity. I ought to be distressed at sleeping during my prayers and acts of thanksgiving. Well, I am not distressed. I think little children please their parents as much when they sleep as when they are awake."[8]

I decided to quote this, because I have found so many, many souls who attribute their dryness and their temptations against the Faith to their lack of fervor, and thus allow their impulse toward Jesus to be broken, although he often permits this to happen in order to immerse them once again in humility and to give them the occasion for this childlike confidence in the simplicity which makes his Heart rejoice.

Thus the vision of her nothingness did St. Thérèse more good than the vision of the Faith.[9] She declared of herself, "the Almighty has done great things in the soul of this child of his heavenly Mother, and the greatest is to have shown her littleness and her powerlessness to her."[10]

You will ask yourself perhaps why I rely so heavily in my preaching on the doctrine of St. Thérèse of the Child Jesus. I do it because I am convinced that she has a great mission in the Church until the end of time, and because I know, by experience, the immense good done in souls by her spirituality. And still more because she has been exalted by our recent popes with an extraordinary forcefulness. And there we are on sure ground.

St. Pius X: "She is the greatest saint of modern times."[11]

Benedict XV: "Here is the secret of sanctity for all the faithful throughout the entire world. She was not, however, nourished by scholarly studies; nevertheless she had so much knowledge by herself that she knew how to show others the true way of salvation. We wish that the secret of holiness of St. Thérèse of the Child Jesus should not remain hidden from a single one of our faithful."¹²

Pius XI: "We fervently desire that all the faithful of
Christ should contemplate her with a view to imitating her.
She acquired such a knowledge of supernatural things that
she was able to chart for others a sure way of salvation.
Everyone must enter into this little way, the way of a gold-
en simplicity, which has nothing childish about it but the
name. . . . What a transformation would come about in the
world if people were to return to this evangelical simplicity.
She was like the living word of God."¹³

Pius XII: "The Lord introduced her into his house, confided to her his secrets, revealed to her all those things which
he hides from the wise and powerful" *(cf. Mt 11:25)*. And
now, after having lived silent and hidden, behold how she
addresses herself to all humanity, to the rich and the poor,
to the great and the humble. It is the Gospel, the heart of
the Gospel, which she has rediscovered. . . . We must take
St. Thérèse at her word when she invites the most unre-
generate as well as the most perfect to count nothing of
value before God save the radical weakness and spiritual
poverty of a sinful creature."¹⁴

John XXIII: "I have a great love for the great Teresa
of Avila, but little Thérèse brings us safe to shore. We must
rely on her."¹⁵

We shall see how "she brings us safe to shore."

Sister Marie of the Sacred Heart, elder sister and god-
mother of St. Thérèse, asked her to put into writing what
she called her "little doctrine." St. Thérèse drew up the
pages where she expresses in admirable terms her immense
desires, feeling in her soul the vocation of warrior, priest,
doctor, martyr, "But," she writes, "I would not know how
to limit myself to one kind of martyrdom; I would have to
have them all."¹⁶

Sister Marie of the Sacred Heart answers her, "I have
read your pages burning with love for Jesus. Your little
Marie is delighted to possess this treasure. Still, a certain
feeling of sadness came over me to see your extraordinary

desire for martyrdom. There, of course, is the proof of your love. Yes, you possess love, but I do not."

Have you never had this feeling of sadness, even perhaps of jealousy, which comes from reading very beautiful things in the lives and writings of saints, with the temptation to say to yourself, "This is not for me; it is too great for me"?

Sister Marie of the Sacred Heart asked Thérèse to tell her whether she could love Jesus as Thérèse did.

Thérèse seized her pen: "I am not at a loss to answer you. . . . How can you ask me if it is possible for you to love God as I love him? My desire for martyrdom is nothing. It is not that which gives me the limitless confidence which I feel in my heart. That desire is a consolation which Jesus sometimes grants to weak souls like mine, but when he does not give this consolation, it is a special grace. . . . Ah, I feel certain that it is not that at all which is pleasing to God in my little soul. What pleases him is to see me love my littleness and my poverty. It is the blind hope which I have in his mercy. . . . There is my only treasure. Why should this treasure not be yours?

"Oh, my darling sister, I beg you, understand your little one. Understand that in order to love Jesus, to be his victim of love, the weaker one is, with neither desires nor virtues, the more one is fit for the workings of this consuming and transforming Love. The sole desire to be a victim suffices, but one must consent to remain always poor and utterly weak.

"Ah, let us stay quite far from all that shines; let us love our littleness, let us love to feel nothing, and we shall then be poor in spirit and Jesus will come to look for us, however far away we are. He will transform us into flames of love. Oh, how I would like to be able to make you understand what I feel. . . . It is confidence and nothing but confidence which must lead us to Love. Does not fear lead us to severe justice such as it is represented to sinners? But it is not this justice which Jesus will have for those who love him."[17]

What a wonderful letter! And how hard it is not to quote the whole of it as I marvel once more at the extraordinary logic of the saints!

Like all theologians, little Thérèse knew that the divine Love is a consuming and transforming love. Therefore, the weaker we are, the more fit we are for the workings of such a love.

To have burning desires, to express them with eloquence, to feel ourselves full of enthusiasm, does not depend directly upon us. What we can always do, however, is to love with our will our littleness and our poverty; we can love our nakedness and our powerlessness and come to have nothing but a single treasure; our blind abandonment to mercy.

That is a program for the interior life which is within your reach.

Do you know what misleads us? The fact that the best men are often so hard. They grow tired of pardoning. They do not forget the wounds they may have received. The world is pitiless in its judgments. It would seem that the perverted should be less severe than others, if only from looking at themselves. Quite the contrary, because mercy is a fruit of grace. Listen to the Pharisees, behind their white-washed façades, passing judgment on the poor publicans.

We apply to the Heart of Jesus the measure of our own miserable little hearts, so mean, so narrow, so hard, and we do not succeed in comprehending how good, how indulgent, how compassionate, how gentle, how patient is Jesus himself.

We are severe particularly through lack of humility. This lack of humility prevents us from going to Jesus with the childlike confidence which permits him to make our hearts gentle and humble like his, to exchange our hearts for his.

Yes, it is really this which misleads us. We have not experienced a truly merciful, universally merciful heart, always benevolent and understanding, which, attracted by misery, always knows how to bend over it in compassion.

Yet that is what the Heart of Jesus is like.

Scripture is full of texts which confirm this doctrine of confidence in misery. I would say of complete confidence in complete misery.

"I will have mercy and not sacrifice" *(Mt 9:13)*. St. Paul writes, "Where sin abounded, grace did more abound" *(Rom 5:20)*. What powerful words: *Copiosa apud eum redemptio (Ps 129:7)*. "With him there is plentiful redemption."

How clearly we see in all this the will of Jesus to save us at all costs. That will made him shed all his blood to the last drop, when a gesture, an absolution would have sufficed. Jesus means Savior. It is his name. And this Savior is always with us, always ready to save us.

He willed to pull Judas from the abyss by gentleness and goodness. At the very moment when Judas betrayed him, he called him his friend: "Friend, do you betray the Son of Man with a kiss?" *(Mt 26:50, Lk 22:48)* The great sin of Judas was not his greed, not even his betrayal: it was his failure to respond to this urgent call from the Heart of Jesus. If at that moment Judas had fallen to his knees saying, "My crime is immense, but your mercy is even greater," Jesus would have taken him in his arms. But Judas doubted that mercy, or he did not want it. That was his downfall.

The great sinners, carried away by their passions, commit their greatest sin, which, it is written, "shall not be forgiven" *(Mt 12:31)* the day they shake off remorse and apostasize through despair and pride, refusing mercy. That is the blasphemy against the Holy Spirit, against Love.

We can go still further. We can base our confidence, not only on the mercy of God, but also on his justice, always following the example of little Thérèse.

"To me," she cries, "he has given his infinite mercy and it is through this that I contemplate and adore the other divine perfections. Then they all appear to me radiant with love. Even justice itself, perhaps even more than anything else, appears to me clothed in love. What a sweet joy to think that God is just, that is to say, that he takes our weaknesses into account, that he knows perfectly the frailty of our nature! Of what, therefore, should I be afraid?"[18]

And to her spiritual brother, Father Roulland: "I know that we must be very pure in order to appear before the God of all holiness, but I know also that the Lord is infinitely just and it is this justice, which terrifies so many souls, which is the object of my joy and confidence. . . . I hope for as much from the justice of God as from his mercy. It is because he is just that he is compassionate and full of gentleness, slow to punish and abounding in mercy, for he knows our frailty. He remembers that we are nothing but dust" *(cf. Ps 102:8).*[19]

And climbing higher: "Since you have loved me to the point of giving your only Son as my Savior and my Spouse, the infinite treasures of his merits are mine. I gladly offer them to you, begging you to look at me only through the face of Jesus and in his Heart burning with love. . . . In the evening of this life I shall appear before you with empty hands, for I do not ask you to count my works. All our justices are stained in your eyes. I want therefore to clothe myself in your own justice and receive from your Love the eternal possession of yourself."[20]

Here is a sublime thought which I expressed to you in my first conference. All the merits of Jesus are mine. He covers me with his blood. He fills my empty hands with his own virtues and transforms me into himself. I present myself thus before the Father and, in all justice, the Father receives me as his beloved Son.

It is in this sense that little Thérèse said: "For the victims of Love, it seems to me that there will be no judgment, but rather that God will hasten to reward with eternal delights his own Love, which he will see burning in their hearts."[21] She knew that "the fire of love is more sanctifying than that of purgatory."

The "little ones" who have surrendered themselves to Love, living here below in the arms of Jesus, on his Heart, will find themselves, at the moment of death, in his arms, on his Heart.

And when Jesus conceals himself during grievous interior trials such as dryness, aridity, anguish in darkness, when all the words of love, confidence, abandonment say nothing more to us, do not touch us, do not reach us any more, what then? What soul has not passed through these nights?

It is then that we must push confidence to the extreme limits. These trials are graces, because they are occasions for pure faith. Pure love is realized in pure faith, and pure faith is realized in darkness in the same way as "strength is perfected in weakness" *(2 Cor. 12:9).* Profit, profit from these dark hours when your nature grieves, when your heart is cold, when you believe, wrongly, that Jesus is very far from you and even, perhaps, that he is turning his eyes away from you, because you see yourself to be so imperfect and wretched; profit from them to make heroic acts of faith and confidence out of pure will. These are the most precious acts—they have immense merit because in those times they are acts of pure faith, without consolation and without sensible aid.

That is the moment to say to Jesus, "You may sleep in my boat, I shall not awaken you. You are hiding yourself, but I know well where you are hidden: you are in my heart. I do not feel it, but I know it. I believe in your love for me and I believe in my love for you."

Throughout the last year of her life, little Thérèse endured this trial of faith and was thus consumed to the very last particle, in the fire of divine Love.

"I would like to be able to express what I feel," she writes, "but alas! I believe that it is impossible. One would have to have traveled in this dark tunnel in order to understand the darkness.

"When I want to rest my heart, fatigued from the darkness which surrounds it, in the memory of the marvelous country toward which I aspire, my torment redoubles. I believe I have made more acts of faith in the last year than during the rest of my life."

But she accepts not being able to enjoy heaven on earth, in order that it may be opened, for all eternity, to the poor unbelievers. "Also," she adds, "in spite of this trial, which takes all enjoyment away from me, I can nevertheless cry out, 'Lord, you fill me with joy in all that you do' *(Ps 91:5).* For is there a joy greater than to suffer for love?"[22]

She thought that Jesus would sooner grow weary of making her wait than she of waiting for him.[23]

And at death? It is said that at the time of death hell is let loose. Jesus can permit it. But is he not near us then, much nearer than Satan? Is not Mary there, supporting this soul which is the stake of the Redemption, with a motherly solicitude? And St. Joseph is there, who knew the sweetness of dying in the arms of Jesus and Mary. Their hearts bend over the dying with an unparalleled saving power at this decisive hour. "Not a single soul falls into hell that has not torn itself out of my arms," said our Lord to a holy soul.

If, according to the Curé of Ars, "It is not the sinner who comes back to God to ask his pardon, but God himself who runs after the sinner and who brings him back to himself,"[24] it is certainly so at the hour of death.

This conference is, I think, the most important one of the retreat. Confidence is the heart of the doctrine of St. Thérèse of the Child Jesus since, "it is confidence and nothing but confidence which will lead us to Love,"[25] and love is everything.

Engrave this in your souls and hearts in letters of gold and fire: immense confidence, unshakeable confidence in this King of Love who is called Jesus—Savior.

Chapter 4

Abandonment

∽∽∽∽∽∽∽∽∽∽∽∽∽∽∽∽∽∽∽∽∽∽∽∽∽∽∽∽∽∽∽∽∽∽∽∽∽

Per ipsum et cum ipso et in ipso: through Jesus, with Jesus, and in Jesus.

"Without me, you can do nothing" *(Jn 15:5)*.

"With you, Jesus, I can do all things" *(cf. Phil. 4:13)*.

Renew these thoughts which bind you to him and which plunge you into the abyss of Love which is his Heart.

The logical and necessary consequence of the complete confidence which I have preached to you until now is total abandonment.

Since it is through Jesus that everything must be accomplished, the more I let him do, the more the work of grace will be beautiful and perfect.

What is this work of grace? The transformation of our souls into Jesus through love. St. Thomas shows us, after St. Augustine, that the Eucharist transforms our souls into Jesus through love.[1] It is there that I find the definition of sanctity, the final word, if I may put it that way, of our divine predestination.

Jesus transforms us into himself; our intelligence is no longer our intelligence, but his: we see things as he sees them. Our will is no longer our will but his: we will what he wills and we reject what he rejects. Our heart is no longer our heart, but the Heart of Jesus: we love what he loves and we detest what he detests.

"And I live, now not I, but Christ lives in me" *(Gal 2:20)*.

Mihi vivere Christus est: "For me, to live is Christ" *(Phil 1:21)*.

Perhaps you will say to me, "You claim that we are continually transformed more and more into him, but I do not notice it, I cannot put my finger on it. And even, some days, seeing myself so miserable, I am tempted to believe the contrary."

Yet, do you not see things more than ever as he does? Of course, you do. Do you not want what he wants, more every day? Of course, you do. I am sure that today, more than ever, you want to love him and make him loved, with a will even more sincere, even more profound, with a desire even more sure than ever, although perhaps not felt. You would not say, "I have less desire to love him and make him loved than yesterday." If that were the case, you would not be here.

What trips us up is that we mistake sensible fervor for sanctity. But it is not. Sanctity is a disposition of soul, animated by grace, which is the life of the soul, under the action of infused virtues and under the influence of the gifts of the Holy Spirit; a disposition to belong to Jesus more than ever, to accomplish his will, to know him and make him known, to love him and make him loved more and more.

He looks much more at what we are than at what we do; and we are, in his eyes, what we sincerely want to be for him.

We understand now why so many Communions—those Communions which transform us into him—do not bring us all the supernatural fruits they could. We open our arms to him, yet we close the doors of our intelligence, of our will, of our heart, by not living in this abandonment. We bid him come, but we do not permit him to enter. But if, in receiving him, we grant him, by perfect abandonment, all the controls, all the keys to the house, that he may be Master in us with full liberty to act, then, oh! what marvels will his omnipotence not accomplish in our souls in the service of his Love!

Abandonment, rightly understood, includes everything. It requires a great humility, since it is submission of oneself to creatures and events, seeing Jesus himself in them. It requires an immense faith, confidence every moment, to tear open the veil of secondary causes, to break through the screen of creatures which too often prevents us from seeing Jesus behind them, who governs everything, since nothing, nothing happens without his having willed or permitted it.

Abandonment is nothing but obedience pushed to its extreme, since it consists of submission to everything within the limits of the possible and the reasonable, in order to obey God who has foreseen and willed it all.

Finally, it is in abandonment that our great desires find their perfect fulfillment. I spoke to you of the splendid passage from little Thérèse where she says that she would have liked to "enlighten souls as did the prophets and doctors, to encircle the earth and announce the Gospel unto the remotest islands, to have been a missionary since the creation of the world and to be one until the consummation of the world, to have suffered all martyrdoms."[2]

She finds the means to realize all that by being the love in the heart of the Church, her Mother. And how was she the love in the heart of the Holy Church? By living in complete conformity with the will of God, who is nothing but Love.

To live with abandonment is to rediscover a perfect harmony in God; for, after all, it is God, it is Jesus, who writes all the lines, all the words, and all the letters of our lives. It is striking to see how the sanctity of all the saints is consummated in total abandonment. All their efforts, all their prayers, all the lights which they have received from heaven, have led them to this.

When our Lord makes some reproach to the saints, to St. Gertrude, to St. Margaret Mary, for example, it is most often their lack of abandonment which he laments. The latter, shortly before her death, wrote that she had finally understood what he expected of her when he said to her, "Let me do it." "His Sacred Heart," she wrote, "will do everything for me if I let him. He shall will, he shall love, he shall desire for me and make up for all my faults."[3]

Like St. Margaret Mary, you may hear Jesus a hundred times a day, saying to you, "Let me do it." In your diffi-

culties, in your problems, in all those things in your daily
life which are sometimes so difficult, so distressing, when
you ask yourself, "What shall I do? How shall I do it?"
listen to him saying to you, "Let me do it." And then
answer him, "O Jesus, I thank you for all things." And it
will be the most beautiful dialogue of love between a soul
and the all-powerful and all-loving God!

Little Thérèse came in this way to the point of no longer
having any other desire than to love Jesus to the point of
"foolishness": "I desire neither suffering nor death, yet I
love both; but it is love alone which attracts me. Now it is
abandonment alone which guides me. I have no other
compass." [4]

"My heart is full of the will of Jesus. Ah, if my soul
were not already filled with his will, if it had to be filled
by the feelings of joy and sadness which follow each other
so quickly, it would be a tide of very bitter sorrow. But
these alternatives do nothing but brush across my soul. I
always remain in a profound peace which nothing can trouble.
If the Lord offered me the choice, I would not choose anything: I want nothing but what he wants. It is what he does
that I love. I acknowledge that it took me a long time to
bring myself to this degree of abandonment. Now I have
reached it, for the Lord took me and put me there." [5]

Yes, I ask the Lord to take you, also, and to put you
there, in the depths of his Heart!

This simple abandonment is the peak of holiness, the
peak of love. When St. Teresa of Avila, in the *Interior
Castle*, speaks of the spiritual marriage, the culminating
point of the mystical life, she depicts it as a union of like-
ness in charity. "Such is the ineffable ardor with which the
souls desire that the will of God be accomplished in them
that they are equally satisfied with anything which it pleases
the Divine Spouse to command." [6]

Practically speaking, of what does abandonment consist?
It consists of seeing the will of God in all that creatures
and events present to you; it is, according to St. Francis

de Sales, to be found in a disposition to ask nothing and to refuse nothing.

Obviously we must reason and judge. We must foresee, make our plans, and act as if all depended on us. I insist upon this because abandonment is neither quietism nor fatalism.

If you have a problem to resolve, you must inform yourself, get to know well the given aspects of the problem, study them, seek the best solution and follow it.

If you are sick, you must call the doctor and follow his prescriptions. In order that no one shall have anything for which to reproach you, you must at least be in total good will.

We must devote ourselves to doing all we have to do, with the greatest fidelity, the greatest generosity, notwithstanding, of course, all our weakness, for we can never say, "I have done all I could." Who can say this besides Mary? We always could have done more. But finally, our task is to have worked with all our good will, in spite of our state of misery, without ever forgetting besides, that Jesus is there to carry us. Then, having acted this way with him, we must never worry over the results. If he wills an apparent failure —I say apparent failure, for a failure willed by God is not a real failure—all is well. "Thank you, Jesus."

If he destroys my little plans, I kiss his adorable hand. It is because he wants to realize his own, which are more beautiful anyway than those which I could have made myself. If he permits a very beautiful success—from my viewpoint— "Thank you again." (That thank you is much easier to say!)

I have sometimes been struck by the sight of very good persons, very pious, heroic in mortification, in austerity, in temperance, refusing the true holocaust, the holocaust which is truly an immolation: the sacrifice of their own will. On one point or another they complain, they worry, and ask something other of the Divine Master than what he has given them. In this they are fleeing from real mortification, in the truest sense of the word.

Jesus always has his victory when he has your abandonment. He needs nothing more than that to bring about the divine wonders that his Heart has prepared for you from all eternity. What spoils everything, what paralyzes him in his providential action on us, is not material difficulties. What can be a material difficulty for him who created heaven and earth? Not his enemies. He will reign despite his enemies. What makes things difficult for him is lack of faith and abandonment on the part of those who call themselves his friends and who ought to be his faithful instruments. We thwart his plans by imposing our own views, our little plans to which we hold so tightly. And, quite often, why do we do it? Through fear of a cross, fear of humiliation, thirst for enjoyment, earthly ambition and, above all, lack of confidence.

Recall the beautiful passage in the Gospel where Jesus says,

"Therefore I say to you, be not solicitous for your life, what you shall eat, nor for your body, what you shall put on. Is not the life more than meat: and the body more than the raiment? Behold the birds of the air, for they neither sow nor do they reap, nor gather into barns: and your Heavenly Father feeds them. Are not you of much more value than they? And which of you by taking thought can add to his stature one cubit? And for raiment why are you solicitous? Consider the lilies of the field, how they grow: they labor not, neither do they spin. But I say to you that not even Solomon in all his glory was arrayed as one of these. And if the grass of the field, which is today, and tomorrow is cast into the oven, God does so clothe, how much more you, oh you of little faith?" *(Mt 6:25 ff.)*

In the same Gospel, it is said, "Seek first the kingdom of God and his justice and all the rest shall be added unto you."

That is what we do not do. We do not seek first the kingdom of God. We seek first our advantage, our interest, money, whatever. And Jesus turns away.

In any case there will be failures, contradictions, very

difficult moments and sometimes very distressing ones. But if there is, on our part, this total confidence which we ought to have in Jesus, he will take care of everything. He will bring good out of evil and even, as I have already told you, a greater good than if there had been no evil; and the trial will have been an immense good for us.

Yes, do everything as if it all depended on you, and leave the result to the Divine Master on whom everything really depends.

When someone asked little Thérèse to summarize her little childlike way she answered: "It is to be disturbed by nothing."[7] I confess that these words say a great deal!

Naturally this means not to be voluntarily disturbed, not consciously or deliberately disturbed, because nature always worries. We worry about everything: the threat of war, political corruption, social relations, family difficulties, children to raise, health, the next day's bread, the future of our loved ones, etc., etc. I who preach confidence at such length spend my time worrying. How can we not ask at every turn, "What is going to happen? How will this turn out?" The main thing is not to consent consciously to anxiety or a troubled mind.

The moment you realize you are worrying, make very quickly an act of confidence: "No, Jesus, you are there: nothing, nothing happens, not a hair falls from our heads, without your permission. I have no right to worry." Perhaps he is sleeping in the boat, but he is there. He is always there. He is all-powerful; nothing escapes his vigilance. He watches over each one of us "as over the apple of his eye" *(Dt 32:10)*. He is all love, all tenderness. It is really an offense against him when we worry voluntarily about anything. That is what causes him pain. That is what wounds his Heart more than anything else.

Such gentle words return constantly to his lips, in an endless refrain which should rejoice our ears and expand our hearts:

Nolite timere. "Do not be afraid. It is I, Jesus" *(Mt 14:27)*.

I emphasize this concept of "worrying with the full consent of the will," for it is very important in the spiritual life to make a distinction between our nature and our will, united to the will of Jesus. "*Homo duplex.*" My nature says, "No," my will says, "Yes." My nature trembles; with all my will, I smile through my tears. My nature is troubled and afraid; my heart recalls the divine testament, "Peace I leave with you, my peace I give unto you" *(Jn 14:27)*. My nature revolts; I force myself to say, "All is well, Jesus, do not change anything." It is a fight which we must take up again and again without ceasing, for our fallen nature always rears up its head. St. Francis de Sales says it dies a quarter of an hour after we do! This is the drama of our life. But the beautiful thing is that Jesus sees our will united to his by a fundamental choice—the profound, habitual disposition of having only one will with him. All those movements of our nature, if we do not consent to them, do not exist for him. There is no sin without consent.

We examine ourselves on our thoughts and our acts; we do not examine ourselves enough on our dispositions toward God and on what he expects of us. This examination will be encouraging, for our good dispositions are sincere and it will reveal the presence in us of "the Holy Spirit poured out into our hearts." Is not a soul in the state of grace his temple and the dwelling place of the Holy Trinity?

It is here that the implacable fight against every unrejected attachment to forbidden things will be decided: against every attachment which (as the very word implies) involves a deliberate and persistent choice, a choice which, however, must not be confused with the possibility of a fall through weakness.

We must not think that sanctity is soaring above temptations, difficulties, and obstacles. No! *De profundis clamavi ad te Domine.* "Out of the depths I have cried to you, O Lord." We live under a Master who died only to rise again, and we possess the hope which is the certainty of his victory, a victory which is ours to the extent that we do not separate ourselves from him.

We can even rejoice, in a sense, in having an evil nature which justly gives us the occasion to deny it our consent and to repeat, "No, Jesus, it is your will that I love; it is that which I want and nothing else. It is you whom I choose."

In the same way as, according to St. Paul, "strength is perfected in weakness" *(2 Cor 12:9)*, confidence is perfected in worry, humility is perfected in the movements of pride, light is perfected in darkness. *Et nox illuminatio mea (Ps 138:2).*

How many times I have heard this statement: "I am a proud person; I am always having thoughts of pride, vanity, self-centeredness, preferring myself to others." I answer, "Are you happy with these thoughts? Do you give them your full consent?" "No, when I notice them, I reject them. I see their inanity, and I am even ashamed of them." "Then you are not a proud person. You have, like me and all of us, a prideful nature. Profit from it to make acts of humility which will put you back in the truth."

The truly proud person is the one who has chosen pride, who has made it the rule of his life, whose avowed goal is not to submit, but to dominate. We are all sinners, and it is necessary for us to recognize it, beating our breast; but the impenitent sinner is the one who has chosen sin.

It is said that the devil makes the gravity of the sin appear to be less during the temptation and greater after the fall. I think this is right. He augments it, not only in order to make the telling of it in the confessional more difficult, but especially in order to discourage us. His plan is to lead souls into despair, as he himself is in despair. His victory is to make us doubt of mercy.

You must believe in mercy to the point of believing that you are a joy for Jesus. I return to this thought which I have already touched upon, for it is essential. The life of the Christian is a life of love. Can people love one another without knowing that they are a joy for each other?

Ask yourself, "How does Jesus see me?" He sees me as

his child since my baptism. He sees me, since my confirmation, filled with the superabundance of the gifts of his
Spirit, marked with the indelible character of a soldier of
his kingdom. He sees married people bathed in the grace
of the sacrament of marriage. And, looking at husband and
wife, he thinks of his union with the Church. He sees me as
his lamb which has so often let itself be led back to the
fold in his arms, purified by absolution. He sees my soul
transformed into himself by Mass and Communion, my soul,
where his Father and he have made their dwelling place
because, "If anyone love me he will keep my word, and my
Father will love him, and we will come to him and will
make our abode with him" *(Jn 14:23)*. These are the actual
realities of sacramental graces!

How many causes of joy for him there are in us! What
more does he see? All you have done for him: your prayers,
your good impulses, all the acts which, in the course of
your lives, have been determined by your faith, your hope,
your love; your acts of generosity, your acts of charity
especially, which you yourselves have forgotten in part but
which he has not forgotten, because they are engraved in
his Heart. On the day of judgment, with what happiness
and what approval he will remind you of all that, in detail,
for his own glory, since he is the author of all that is good,
but for yours, also, because you will have believed in his
love. "Come, you blessed of my Father" *(Mt 25:34)*.

And if, in addition to all that, you give him your many
miseries with great humility, but also great confidence,
then you give him his great joy—his joy of being Savior.
Every soul in a state of grace is for him a heaven which
only that soul could give him.

Here is a good resolution to take from the retreat: "I
promise you, Jesus, to worry about nothing consciously,
voluntarily, deliberately. As soon as I notice myself worrying, I shall listen to your gentle voice saying to me, 'Let me
do it. Am I not here with you, in you?' and I shall say
unconditionally 'O Jesus, I thank you for everything,' for

you always expect that of me."

Abandonment is a practical and actual application of an obsession: the will of God. That is why certain persons in the world, men of the people, this peasant on his farm, that worker in the factory, are true saints—because they have understood that the will of God is everything and they are disposed to prefer it to everything else. From the moment when I am in the will of God, everything is fine. This is where the supernatural indifference of the saints comes from: joy or pain, consolation or dryness, light or darkness, adulation or criticism, honey or gall, health or sickness, life or death. *Ecce ancilla Domini.* "Behold the handmaid of the Lord." *Fiat voluntas tua.* "Thy will be done." *Sit nomen Domini benedictum.* "Blessed be the name of the Lord." That sums up the sanctity of the Blessed Virgin.

Remember that each event in your life brings you Jesus' will, which is Jesus himself. It is he whom you can embrace in everything that comes to you. I bless him, therefore, however my nature may protest. It will protest. There will be interior seething; there will be revolt of the senses; there will be moaning. But I shall bless him for everything, with all my will, united to his. I shall say in union with Mary, *"Fiat! Magnificat!"* in the midst of the tempest, and thus I shall always have a heavenly peace in the depths of my soul.

The peace will perhaps not be felt; it will be the peace of which St. Paul speaks, "which passes all understanding" *(Phil 4:7).*

You see that this doctrine is not simply one of letting things be. Far from it! Moreover, the tender Master who knows the price of the cross and the thorns, will know how to be considerate toward you. He will permit plenty of humiliations and plenty of deceptions. He will destroy many false dreams. The Divine Surgeon will put the lancet straight into the abscess, happy that you allow him to do it. But do not be afraid—no, do not be afraid! His hand is very gentle,

very skillful, moved by his Heart which loves you to the
point of foolishness, and the awakening will be very beautiful! To abandon yourself thus to Jesus is to permit him to
carry out his whole work of love. He wants us to follow
him, the King, crucified and crowned with thorns, even to
Calvary—but also to the Resurrection, to his heaven of
glory!

Faith, for you, the privileged of his Heart, does not
consist solely in believing in the mystery of the Holy Trinity
or in the Real Presence in the tabernacle, in never doubting
a dogma of the Holy Church. No, that is not a sufficient
faith for you. Faith, for you, is to believe without seeing it,
that Jesus is always near you, with you, guiding everything,
always respecting your liberty, for his greater glory and
your glory in his. Believe in the dogma of Love!

Do I know by myself what is best for me? My views are
so short-sighted, my horizon so limited! I let the Divine
King decide. He sees better and further than I and he does
not have to ask me my opinion.

Jesus told St. Gertrude who asked him to heal one of her
friends, "You trouble me, Gertrude, by asking me for the
cure of your friend. I sent her this sickness as a trial. She
accepts it with admirable submission to my will which gains
great merit for her, and I thus prepare a more beautiful
heaven for her for all eternity." That does not mean that
we must not pray, and with all our hearts, for the healing
of the sick, but always with the thought that if Jesus does
not grant it, it is because his plan is more beautiful than
ours.

St. Augustine relates in his *Confessions*[8] that when he
lived in Carthage with his parents, he made the decision
to go to Rome to teach. Augustine was not a saint at that
time, but a great libertine. His mother, who wanted nothing
but the salvation of his soul, thought that this departure,
which took her son away from her influence in order to ex-
pose him to all the temptations of Rome, would be the end of
all her hopes. But Augustine relates: "Why I left the one

country and went to the other, you knew, O God, but you did not tell either me or my mother. She indeed was in dreadful grief at my going and followed me right to the seacoast. There she clung to me passionately, determined that I should either go back home with her or take her to Rome with me, but I deceived her with the pretence that I had a friend whom I did not want to leave until he had sailed off with a fair wind. . . . She would not return home without me, but I managed with some difficulty to persuade her to spend the night in a place near the ship where there was an oratory in memory of St. Cyprian. That night I stole away without her; she remained praying and weeping. And what was she praying for, O my God, with all those tears but that you should not allow me to sail! But you saw deeper and granted the essential part of her prayer: you did not do what she was at that moment asking, that you might do the thing she was always asking."

Monica was opposed to his departure, but it was in Italy that Augustine was to encounter St. Ambrose who was the instrument of his conversion.

Thus, as St. Augustine said, God refused to grant St. Monica the prayer she prayed on that day, in order to grant her the prayer she prayed every day. Her prayer on that particular day was, "Let him not leave!" Her prayer of every day: "Let him be converted! Let him be converted!" Yet it was necessary for him to leave in order that he might be converted. This happens so often in our lives, doesn't it? We ask, without knowing it, for the very thing which is the contrary of our greatest good, of our true happiness.

The following objection is sometimes made: In the Gospel it is said, "Ask and it shall be given you, seek and you shall find, knock and it shall be opened to you" *(Lk 11:9).*

We certainly can ask for material and earthly things, and if we ask with confidence, Jesus is touched and very often grants them to us, for he loves so much to please and satisfy his children. But it is more beautiful to ask for nothing in the temporal order except with this condition: "If it is in your loving plan for us, Jesus."

In the spiritual order, we may always ask, I dare to say, insist, when we are sure that it is the divine will. For example, for peace in the world, or for a conversion. But here again, we must leave to Jesus "his hour" for the realization of our prayer.

For temporal things, it is more beautiful to leave it up to him. "Take care of my interests," he said to St. Margaret Mary, "and I shall take care of yours." When the apostles said to him, "Lord, teach us to pray" *(Lk 11:1)*, he taught them the Our Father.

Hallowed be thy name, thy kingdom come, thy will be done. Give us this day our daily bread—yes, included is the bread that is necessary in order to live on this earth; but the daily bread refers, above all, to the Eucharist, and to the bread of which he spoke when he said, "My bread is to do the will of my Father" *(cf. Jn 4:34)*.

Deliver us from evil. "But would you not also like this or that? The end of a certain trial? the success of an enterprise?" "Lord, your will be done, your kingdom come." "And for those you love, what do you ask me?" "Lord, that they may hallow your name, that they may do your will, that your kingdom may come in them and through them."

Do you not believe that if you pray in this way, with such a faith, such a reliance on Love, Jesus will always give you what is best both for you and for those you love? "The hundredfold here below" *(Mt 19:29)*, quite aside from the eternal happiness, of which St. Paul says, like Isaias, "Eye has not seen, nor ear heard, neither has it entered into the heart of man, what things God has prepared for them who love him" *(1 Cor 2:9)*.

Those who are generous in abandonment awake to marvelous vistas. After the days of storms and darkness, when Jesus lifts the veil and reveals a little of what he has done for him who has believed (he will not show it fully except in heaven—that will be our heaven), what joy to be able to say, "Oh, how right I was to believe! I believed and he surpassed all my hopes."

We only saw the links in the chain one by one, without seeing how they are interconnected. The day Jesus allows you to catch a glimpse of the whole golden chain, the marvelous succession of events, you will thank him and bless him. And what is incomparably more beautiful is to thank him and bless him before having seen—breaking through misleading appearances by these words alone:

"I do not see, but I am sure of you, I believe because I know who you are, I know whom I have believed." *Scio cui credidi (2 Tim 1:12).*

On the other hand, those who have been lax, who have complained, protesting and attempting to escape the trial, who have revolted or cried, "Lord, Lord, save me," like St. Peter sinking in the waves, will find themselves covered with confusion. They will hear Jesus say to them, "Men of little faith! You doubted, you feared as if I were not there, or as if I did not love you."

However, there again there is a remedy, so great is the mercy of the Heart of Jesus. It is to offer him with confidence, as little Thérèse did, our lack of confidence, and to offer him with peace our lack of peace. Nothing is irreparable with Jesus.

Therefore, the conclusion is to let him do as he wills. He is the pilot. The oarsmen turn their backs to the goal while rowing; the pilot sees. He is the one who steers the boat. Let us row with all our strength and let Jesus guide us into port.

St. Bernard preached a Crusade and the Crusade failed. St. Alphonsus was expelled from the congregation he had founded. There are many, many examples of this kind in the course of the centuries. There is the "failure" of Calvary. Jesus came to earth to establish his Church. He formed his apostles, with so much care and pain, to be its pillars. At Gethsemane they all fled. At Calvary they were all absent except John, and yet there was Jesus, himself, dying on the Cross. It was the failure of failures. Everything seemed absolutely finished. Recall the sadness of the disciples at Emmaus, because they had not had enough faith, in spite of the Scriptures, to see in this failure the marvelous victory that it really was: the prelude to the Resurrection. This failure of failures was the victory of victories!

In our defeats, whatever they are, we can see the victory of Jesus, and therefore our own victory in him, when we accept them in the certainty that he has permitted them in wisdom and in love for us. We say, "I have struggled, I have taken so much trouble, I have made so many efforts—all to arrive at what? Nothing—or sometimes at a great humiliation." The *Magnificat* which you sing in your disappointment, the "Thank you for everything" which you say in your humiliation, is the most beautiful of all successes, the most fruitful of all victories.

If you live this teaching, you will have the heroism of the theological virtues, which are the highest virtues—a heroism of which Jesus will be the real hero, since without him we can do nothing (*cf. Jn 15:5*). "Jesus, be in me the hero of the heroism of the virtues. I myself am nothing but weakness, misery, and impotence, but I have given you my heart, my will, my intelligence, so you will do it all. It is for this that you came to earth: to do, yourself, in us, all that you ask of us, according to the beautiful prayer, 'We pray you Lord, let our actions be prompted by your inspiration and furthered by your help, so that all our prayers and all our acts may begin from you, and through you he accomplished.'"[9]

Our collaboration consists, above all, in our faith, our hope, and our love, our good will in humility, our grateful abandonment.

Father de Caussade (Pierre de Caussade, S. J.), in his beautiful book on abandonment, as relevant today as two centuries ago, remarks that, "God still speaks to souls as he spoke to them in the time when there were neither

directors nor methods of perfection. Fidelity to the will of
God was the whole of spirituality; the faithful saw that
each moment brings a duty to fulfill with fidelity and love.
All attention was focused successively on each new duty.
The faithful spirit, moved continually by the divine impulse,
was turned toward the new topic which presented itself
through God, according to God, at each moment.

"It is thus that Mary was content to say to the Angel,
'*Fiat mihi secundum verbum tuum,*' 'Be it done to me according to your words,' an expression of the most simple
abandonment of the soul to the will of God, in whatever
form it may be presented. And it was thus that Jesus taught
us to say with him, '*fiat voluntas tua,*' 'your will be done,'
as the most perfect of prayers.

"As we know that the divine action encompasses everything, guides everything, does everything except sin, it is a
duty of faith to adore it in everything, to love it and receive it with open arms, with joy and confidence, rising always above appearances which, by their very obscurity,
bring about the triumph of faith.

"The will of God is itself the better part. There is nothing
more to do than to let it act and abandon ourselves to it,
blindly, with perfect confidence. There is the mustard seed
whose fruits we do not gather because we do not recognize
them in their littleness. There is the drachma of the Gospel,
the treasure which we do not find because we suppose it to
be too far away to seek.

"Do not ask me what the secret is for finding this treasure. There is no secret. The treasure is everywhere. It is
offered to us at all times, in all places. Creatures, friends
and enemies, pour it out openhandedly and let it flow through
all the faculties of our bodies and souls to the center of our
hearts. Let us open our mouths and they shall be filled.
Divine action inundates the universe, it penetrates all creatures, it hovers over them: everywhere they are, it is there.
It goes before them, accompanies them and follows them.
We have nothing to do but to let ourselves be carried by

its waves.

"How I desire," Father de Caussade exclaims in conclusion, "how I desire, O my God, to be the missionary of
this holy will, to teach the whole world that there is nothing
so easy, so common, or so accessible to everyone as holiness."[10]

Frequently make what I call the examination of the prayer
"O Jesus, I thank you for everything." It should be the fruit
of your disposition of will, of heart, and of soul to bless
Jesus for everything that he wills or permits for you, for
everything that happens to you. Promise always to say to
him, "I thank you for everything." You may answer, "I
am going to make this promise, but I know that I shall not
keep it. After a trial, a contradiction, a humiliation, in trouble, I shall not think to say it; or, if I think of it, I shall
perhaps not have the courage; or again, feeling my nature
in revolt, it will seem like a lie to say, 'Thank you.'"

All right, then! Promise him, at the same time, to say
thank you for not having said thank you right away. It is
still another humiliation, a lack of courage, a misery to offer
him with humility and confidence.

In this short and simple prayer there is at the same time
humility, an immense confidence in merciful love, abandonment, and thanksgiving. How rich this little prayer is! How
it glorifies Jesus and how it pleases him! Each time you say
it, it reaffirms your disposition of love for him in total
abandonment. It sinks you into his Heart, for it sings of his
love for you. It is nothing other than the *gratias agentes
semper pro omnibus*, "giving thanks always for all things,"
of St. Paul *(Eph 5:20)*. What St. Paul asked of the Ephesians, I can certainly ask of you. I have known persons for
whom this prayer has become the breathing of their souls,
and who have thus climbed very high in love. "O Jesus, I
thank you for everything." If you were to retain nothing
but that from this retreat, it would be a great thing.

Do not believe those who suppose and say that abandonment is only for advanced souls. Advanced or not, I was.

created and put into the world to love God who loved me first. "The one who loves me," said Jesus, "is the one who loves my will." Abandonment is nothing but that.

During my long life as a priest, I have had to guide many souls, men and women of all ages, children and adults, from all backgrounds: intellectuals and those with little education, priestly souls, consecrated souls, persons from all classes, rich and poor. I have found them all open to this doctrine, receiving it as the earth in springtime drinks the dew from heaven.

This doctrine can be adapted to various situations, but it is always the same; the Gospel, in its divine simplicity, is for everyone. It is neither a theory nor a theological demonstration. It is a way of life.

"I am come that they may have life and may have it more abundantly" *(Jn 10:10)*.

"I am the bread of life" *(Jn 6:35)*.

"For the life was manifested; and we have seen and do bear witness, and declare unto you that everlasting life which was with the Father, and has appeared to us" *(1 Jn 1:2)*.

Chapter 5

Great Desires, Humility, Peace

In order to give Jesus love for Love, we must be souls of desire. Nothing great ever comes about without great desires. They are the mainspring, the driving force. If they are lacking everything is dull and lifeless. We must desire to be not only good, but holy. Perhaps you will not know how to express these desires with ardor; the essential thing, however, is that you be filled with them.

Observe how in things of this world, things of earth, desires lie behind great successes. A businessman who wants to make money makes his plans and prepares his publicity in order to earn more. A painter who wants to succeed at the exhibition comes back to his painting and retouches it again and again. I knew a very great organist who, when he was preparing for the conservatory competition, spent entire nights at his pedal board. In the morning, he couldn't even walk over to his bed!

What will men not do to gain public recognition? How many steps—and sometimes, how many compromises! Yet all that is for a temporary fortune, a fleeting enjoyment, for the glory of a moment, a puff of smoke.

And you, called to partake in the intimate life of the Holy Trinity, to know God as he knows himself, to love him as he loves himself—how sad it would be if you were merely to creep along in indifference! Routine, terrible routine is the daughter of apathy.

In order to rise out of mediocrity and lukewarmness, renew your desires.

"If anyone thirsts, let him come to me; let him drink who believes in me" *(Jn 7:37)*.

"To him who thirsts, I will give the fountain of the water of life, freely" *(Ap 21:6)*.

69

Oh, tell Jesus that you thirst—that you thirst for him! The great commandment, "You shall love the Lord your God with your whole heart, and with your whole soul, and with all your strength, and with all your mind" *(Lk 10:27)*, is not reserved to Trappists or Carmelites. It is for everyone.

Here again, it is the Master who gave us the example. He himself, first of all, was the man of desires.

Desiderio desideravi, "With desire I have desired to eat this Pasch with you before I suffer" *(Lk 22:15). Sitio*, "I thirst"—I thirst for your souls, I thirst for your hearts, I thirst for your sanctification. You whom I have filled, quench my thirst for love by your thirst to love me. "I have come to cast fire on the earth. And what will I, but that it be kindled" *(Lk 12:49)*.

Let your desire to love him, to be one with him, be the response to his own desire to be yours.

The saints who have risen very high in heaven arrived there on the wings of great desires. St. Mary Magdalen dei Pazzi had a vision one day of the glory of St. Louis Gonzaga. She was astonished: "How did this youth rise so high among the Seraphim?" It was revealed to her that he had attained this glory because, during his short life, he was consumed with the desire to love God and to be a saint.

I must add, that to desire to love is already to love. A great desire to love is already a great love. In the same way that Jesus said to St. Augustine, "You would not seek me if you had not already found me," he will say to you, "You would not have this great desire to love me if you did not love me already." He cannot fail to fulfill, beyond even our greatest hopes, a desire that he himself has inspired.

Along with these great desires, keep a profound, convinced, sincere sense of your weakness and impotence. Perhaps you will tell me, "You want us to fly very high in the heaven of divine love, yet the first thing we must do is to admit that we have no wings." Well, are you going to become distressed? to despair? Many do.

How many souls I have met who have experienced these

beautiful enthusiasms, yet, in admitting their weakness, their apparent mediocrity, their lack of progress, have let themselves little by little be overrun by discouragement. They say, "Holiness is not for me. I believed it was, I wanted it, but I must come down a peg." And the devil seizes on this and profits by such an abdication to make them give up the fight, and to break down every good impulse.

Do not fall into this snare. Rather renew your desires with the tremendous confidence that I preached to you in the first conferences: renew them on a foundation of profound humility.

In one of his discourses addressed to Lisieux[1] Pius XII said, "We would like in a few words to interpret the fervor and admiration of everyone toward St. Thérèse of the Child Jesus. If Divine Providence permitted the extraordinary diffusion of her cult, is it not because she transmitted and still transmits to the world a message of astonishing spiritual penetration, a witness of unique humility, confidence, and love?" And speaking of the message of humility the Holy Father adds,

"After having lived silent and hidden, she now addresses all humanity, the rich and the poor, the great and the humble. She tells them as Christ did, 'Enter in at the narrow gate: for wide is the gate, and broad is the way that leads to destruction, and many there are who go in thereat; but narrow is the gate, and straight is the way that leads to life: and few there are that find it'" *(Mt 7:13).*

You will perhaps be astonished that after having preached to you that confidence which so enlarges the soul and expands the heart, I should speak to you about the narrow gate on the subject of the "little way." But listen to the Holy Father: "The gate which is truly narrow, accessible to all, is that of humility." The narrow way, the narrow gate, is for those who become again like little children.

To his disciples who asked him who was the greatest in the Kingdom of Heaven, Jesus, calling a little child and placing him in the midst of them, answered,

"Amen I say to you, unless you be converted, and become as little children, you shall not enter into the Kingdom of Heaven. Whoever therefore shall humble himself as this little child, he is the greatest in the Kingdom of Heaven" *(Mt 18:1-4)*.

What are we? Feeble creatures, worse than nothing because we are sinners. We have received everything. God has created us and, moreover, he must keep us in existence because, if he forgot us for an instant, left to ourselves we would return to nothingness.

If the proud person could only see how ridiculous he is, as well as guilty, when he flings his defiance at God! One little vessel breaks in our brain, and our life is finished.

Face to face with God we have not a single right, yet this expression, "my rights," comes so easily! We have a thirst for esteem which is never quenched. These obvious truths remain practically hidden from us. Right reason grasps them, but in the habitual practice of our thoughts, blinded as we are by our passions, our interests, the love of ourselves, we forget our absolute creaturely dependence. This is because we do not look at the things we do not like to see. We do not like these truths; yet, when we look them in the face with the eyes of the Divine Master, what peace we shall find in them!

The saints learned to rejoice in humility and humiliations, for humility and love of humiliations are of a piece. I speak here, obviously, of a love that is of pure will, for our fallen nature does not seek humiliations, or love them. Our nature detests them.

As far as I know, there is nothing more repugnant to us, which has a more deathly taste, than humiliation. It truly is a taste of death, since it is what makes us die to ourselves. It kills us by making us smaller in the eyes of others and in our own eyes.

Contempt, and indifference even more than contempt, is hard to accept. We must swallow the bitter gall of being left aside as insignificant while the idol of self is obliged to bow its head. But in this taste of death for our nature, there is also a taste of divine life, because it is in the measure that we die to ourselves that we live in God, that Jesus takes a greater place in us.

St. Francis of Assisi, imagining that on arriving at the monastery with little Brother Leo they would not be received, that the porter would not open the door for them, that he would leave them outdoors in the snow, or worse than that, that he would chase them away, cudgeling them with sticks, said to the little brother, "That would be perfect joy!" And that is but little compared to what I would call the cudgeling of the soul: the lack of esteem, the ironies, the injustices of those with whom we live, whom we love, yet who nevertheless humiliate us, often without intending it.

Since the fall, we are all proud men. We want to dominate, we want to command, we want to be appreciated, we want to be applauded. Contempt and indifference leave a profound sadness, a painful bitterness in our souls.

The apostles at the Last Supper, after three years of life near our Lord, still disputed among themselves as to which of them was the greatest *(cf. Lk 22:24).*

What a contrast with Jesus! We spoke of his follies of love. Why were they follies of love? Because they were follies of humility and annihilation.

Bethlehem: the infinite God, a little child on the straw of a manger. Nazareth: a poor God, a God who is an apprenticed worker, whom those near him, his own, treated as a visionary! He was with his apostles as one who serves and not as one who is served. The washing of the feet: Jesus on his knees before Judas, humbly and carefully washing his feet. Gethsemane: when he appeared before his Father covered with all the sins of men. The festival robe in which Herod clothed him in mockery. Barabbas preferred to him. Raised on the cross, with two thieves beside him: God, put on the level of criminals. The cruel irony hurled at him when he was on the cross: "He saves others and cannot save himself. Come down if you can." And finally, the Tabernacle until the end of time.

I assure you that it will help you more than anything else when you are forsaken, wrongly judged, calumniated, rejected, to think of his humiliations. When you are suffering under the blow of a humiliation, think of those he endured. He was not obliged to suffer them, but he knew how hard it would be for us to be humiliated, so he himself willed to be the first to show us the way, in order to be able to say to us, "Where I have passed you can pass too." This is all the more true because we do not walk in his footsteps, but are carried by him.

He was infinite innocence and purity. We are all guilty. Whatever be the injustice which falls on us, we can always tell ourselves that we have merited it, if not at the present time (since I have called it an injustice), at least by our past faults.

To practice this is a difficult thing: not to protest, not to take offense, not to complain. Under the pretext of dignity, of justice, what hindrances we place in the way of humility! The majority of hurts, offended feelings, grudges, bitternesses in life with others, come from this obsession with our rights, this need for esteem, so strongly woven into our "self." He who honestly puts himself in the last place is not astonished when others put him there too.

"Every one who exalts himself shall be humbled; and he who humbles himself shall be exalted" *(Lk 14:11)*.

If we knew all we gain by humiliations, we would thirst for them. Besides, no one but disciples of Jesus can be humble. There is no humility without his grace. It does not exist in the world because it is too contrary to our nature, wounded by the sin of pride.

"For God resists the proud" *(1 Pt 5:5)*—terrible words! But he delivers himself up, he gives himself totally to the humble and the small. He surrenders to them. Not only does he not resist them, but he cannot refuse them anything, as was the case with the woman of Canaan *(cf. Mt 15:28)*.

He prefers the poor, the disgraced, the destitute, the needy, because they are generally more humble. He preferred the Curé of Ars, the little Bernadette, who said that if the Holy Virgin had found a child at Lourdes more poor and ignorant than she, it would have been that child whom she would have chosen. The same was true at La Salette, at Pontmain, at Fatima. As a schoolboy, St. Pius X went barefoot from his home to school, his shoes over his shoulder, in order not to wear them out.

"I offer praise to you, Father, Lord of heaven and earth, because you have hidden these things from the wise and the prudent, and have revealed them to little ones" *(Lk 10:21)*. We sense that this cry of Jesus comes from the very depths of his heart. St. Luke tells us that in pronouncing these words, "He rejoiced in the Holy Spirit." He foresaw at this moment the army of little souls, the marvelous army of the "very small," called to reconquer the world for his Heart: *revelasti parvulis* "you have revealed them to the little ones."

The humble man realizes that he does nothing good in the supernatural order by himself; that applause is bad for him—it seems to him that it is a sort of stealing. All good comes from the beloved King, evil from himself. This is justice and truth. He realizes it with joy and peace. With the same simplicity, thinking of the graces he has received, he will say, *Fecit mihi magna qui potens est. (Lk 1:49)* By myself I can do nothing, but "he who is all-powerful has done great things in me."

"Let us remain very remote from all that glitters," wrote little Thérèse. "Let us love our littleness; let us love to feel nothing. Then we shall be poor in spirit and Jesus will come seeking us, however far away we are. He will transform us into flames of love!"[2]

Humility is an abyss which attracts torrents of graces, which attracts Jesus himself into a soul. He was not able to resist the humility of the prodigal son, the good thief, the woman of Canaan. The vacuum which humiliation makes

in us when we receive it rightly is an emptiness which attracts him irresistibly. He bends over the soul who loves its
littleness and nothingness, he bends over it with an unspeakable love.

So be humble before God. Everything is a gift on his part
—a gratuitous gift. Even after the most beautiful acts of
generosity, you can say truthfully, "I am an unprofitable
servant" *(Lk 17:10).*

Be humble before the authority which represents God on
earth. Be humble also before yourself. Often we are sad-
dened here by the very thing which will be the cause of
our eternal happiness above.

How many women have gone astray because of their
physical beauty! How many men because of their brilliant
intelligence, their talent, their eloquence! I think of that when
I meet a homely person who, throughout her whole life, has
never seen a look of admiration or interest resting on her
because she is ugly or infirm. And I look at her and say
to myself, "How beautiful she will be in heaven! If she could
only see the look of tenderness Jesus gives her simply because she is counted for nothing by those for whom only
the success of this world counts. If she knew how to accept
with faith and love what God has chosen for her, what glory
she would have above! What would these few years which
she will have passed neglected on earth seem like to her
then? A very little trial compared to the splendor with which
she shall shine in the radiance of a paradise without end. 'So
shall the last be first'" *(Mt 20:16).* Opium of the people?
No: divine and eternal reality.

This does not mean that those who have received natural
gifts ought not to rejoice in them. These gifts are a part of
our predestination; they are in the plan of God's love for
us. Some great saints have been abundantly gifted. St.
Augustine and St. Thomas were geniuses. St. Teresa of
Avila was beautiful, a marvel of natural grace and wit;
St. Francis de Sales, an exquisite being with refinement
of intelligence and delicacy of heart and manners. But I

think that these gifts served especially to help them fulfill their special mission in the Church, and that they were saints in the measure to which they realized the gratuitousness of the gifts and their own fundamental poverty. St. Thomas considered all his theological works as "straw."

To be humble in accepting our lack of success. The intoxication of praise, of adulation, turns a person's head, sometimes to the point of dizziness. When everything is successful, when a person receives nothing but applause, how could he not believe himself to be something or someone important? That is the danger of prominent positions. Therefore bless the humiliation which disillusions and which saves. We must strive to be humble in accepting our mistakes, to know how to say, "I was wrong." It is not easy; it costs something. To know how to hold ourselves in contempt, to seek counsel and, at the same time, not to be preoccupied with the opinion of creatures, with what people will say. When we decide on some action, nine times out of ten we keep asking ourselves, "What are people going to think? What will so-and-so think if I do that?" and not, "What will Jesus think?"

I have often seen souls paralyzed by a small humiliation. This soul cannot bear the slightest pin-prick while that one cannot stand a contradiction, and chasms are thus created between souls. Each one shuts himself up in his revolt, and bitterness spreads in his heart.

Another consequence of offended self-love is getting all upset. After a man falls, and sees himself on the ground, then, rather than simply recognizing his own weakness and impotence, and remaining in peace, he concludes, "I shall never succeed. I give up. It is useless." That is really rebellious discouragement. The one who is truly childlike is not surprised that he stumbles. He falls and picks himself up again without wearying, each time more determined to attain his goal.

A ravishing form of humility is simplicity. It is the charm of those who know how to put themselves in their proper place and are not puffed up in their own eyes. Have you noticed that to say of someone that he is simple is the praise which crowns all others? "There is a remarkable man!" people will say. "What intelligence, what erudition, what authority, and . . . he is so simple!"

Simplicity creates an agreeable atmosphere for everyone, puts people at their ease, brings hearts back together. This is because it presupposes a true forgetfulness of self. The simplicity of Pope John XXIII explains in great part his astonishing worldwide radiance.

"Blessed are the meek, for they shall inherit the earth" *(Mt 5:4)*. An inexhaustible theme of meditation is the simplicity of the Holy Family: of Jesus, Mary, and Joseph.

The spirit of obedience is a subject appropriate to a chapter on humility, and I shall undertake to talk to you about it, for it is not a virtue reserved to religious. It is the great lesson of Jesus, and therefore it is a lesson for everyone.

What do we see at the origin of this folly of Love, the Incarnation? Obedience: *Ecce venio ut faciam, Deus, voluntatem tuam:* "Behold I come . . . it is written of me, that I should do your will, O God" *(Heb 10:7)*.

In the very consummation of the Redemption what do we again find? Obedience: *Factus obediens usque ad mortem:* "He humbled himself, becoming obedient unto death" *(Phil 2:8)*.

If we search the Gospel to find what the life of God incarnate on earth was for thirty years, we find the answer in three words: *Erat subditus illis,* "(He) was subject to them" *(Lk 2:51)*. Seated on the edge of Jacob's well he said to his disciples, "My meat is to do the will of Him, who sent me" *(Jn 4:34)*. What strong words: "My meat. . . ."

The Word became flesh. He shed his blood to the last drop in order to save us. Yes, that is true; but he did this in order to obey his Father, and by this loving obedience to carry out the immolation of his sacrifice.

"If any man will come after me, let him deny himself, and take up his cross, and follow me" *(Mt 16:24)*.

"Unless the grain of wheat falling into the ground die, it remains alone" *(Jn 12:24)*.

What within ourselves is most intimately ours? Our own will: that is the center of our person. To die to ourselves, is to die to what we cling to most: our own will. Only obedience can bring about in us this crucifixion and this liberation. Psichari said, "We are among those who burn to obey, in order to be free."

We owe obedience to God, to the Holy Church, to the hierarchy. But St. Paul specifies even further: "Let women be subject to their husbands. . . . Children, obey your parents. . . . Servants, be obedient to those who are your lords according to the flesh" *(Eph 5 and 6)*. He gives us the great supernatural motive for this submission: that women may see in their husbands, children in their parents, and servants in their masters, the Lord himself. Then he hastens to exhort husbands to love their wives as Christ loves the Church, parents not to provoke their children to anger, and masters to leave aside threatenings and remember that the master who is in heaven is their master too. Reread these chapters, the fifth and sixth in the epistle to the Ephesians; they are marvelously practical.

One thing is certain: God could not have failed to provide his creatures with a way by which to go to him, to come to the knowledge of the true religion.

We can say with equal certainty that this way is sure. How is this way of salvation, which is the Church, assured? By obedience to external authority.

God speaks to us in two ways: he speaks in the intimacy of the mind and heart by interior lights, by touches of his grace, by good inspirations, by holy desires, and he speaks externally by visible legitimate authority. If there is conflict between the two, which must take precedence? Which will be the will of God? Always and everywhere the word of the external authority.

All the security of the children of the Church comes from that. At first glance it would seem that it would be better

to obey an interior voice which would be the direct voice of
God, but it is not that way. The miracle is in fact much
greater than if God had decided to guide us directly. He did
not will to do that, doubtless so that we would rely more on
faith. Thus things have the appearance of operating humanly;
but they are actually all the more divine.

How amazing is this omnipotence of God who, in respecting the liberty of each of us, will never hold against us an
act of submission to an intermediary designated by himself.

It is Jesus who will give you this humility and submission
in the measure that you desire them and ask for them, with
confidence, in your prayers.

Let a conference like this one not discourage you in any
respect by making you say, "I have so much self-love, I
am not submissive, I always have thoughts of pride, I surprise myself again and again by preferring myself to others.
I cling to my will. In everything, or almost everything, you
say about the person who is preoccupied with himself, I
recognize myself. I am what you say we must not be."

I hear, I sense these complaints of your nature. They are
right; they plunge you into a profound truth—the fact of
your wretchedness. They bring you face to face with your
nature, wounded by the sin of our first parents who wanted
to be "like gods" *(Gn 3:5)*—a grave wound, made by pride
and refusal of love.

But it is here that you must recall what I have already
told you—that it is consent that makes the sin. To have a
proud nature and to be a proud person are not the same
thing. Once again, the truly proud man is the one who takes
pleasure in his pride, who sees no evil in it, who thinks he
does not need mercy, and refuses it. This is not the case
with you, who do not consent to it, especially since you
believe in Jesus who repairs, who purifies, who only permits
evil in order to draw from it a greater good, in Jesus who
cures and who saves, in Jesus who loves you. It could be a
very fruitful humiliation to recognize your pride without
consenting to it.

What will crown this humility, this confidence, this abandonment which I have preached to you up till now? The
peace which Jesus came to bring upon the earth.

That was his first gift to men. Even before he spoke, in
his eagerness to make us the gift of his Heart, he sent his
angels to announce a surpassing joy to all people:

"For this day is born to you a Savior, who is Christ the
Lord. . . . You shall find the infant wrapped in swaddling
clothes and laid in a manger. . . . Glory to God in the
highest, and on earth, peace to men of good will" *(Lk 2:10-
14)*. That was his first gift of love. That was his last. At
the Cenacle, before leaving his apostles, he left them a heritage: "Peace I leave with you, my peace I give unto you"
(Jn 14:27). That is his testament.

This peace comes through fidelity to grace, fidelity to
confidence. It gives sweetness to your intimacy with Jesus.
To lose confidence is to draw back from his arms, and at
the same time it is to lose peace.

The fruit of this peace is supernatural calm. The devil
fishes in troubled waters. Whoever lets himself be troubled
does not see clearly any more, stumbles, falls into a panic,
ceases to judge rightly. We can be very shaken, very upset,
as long as it is only on the surface, but the depths of our
souls must remain tranquil as the depths of the ocean, even
during the greatest storms.

Weep in bereavement or misfortune, but weep in peace.
You may lose everything, but you do not have the right to
lose your peace.

Be peaceful in the failures of your spiritual life, peaceful
in the failures of your apostolate. You spend yourself, you
devote yourself, you almost kill yourself, often to arrive at
the most disappointing results. You sow, others will reap.
You will reap in heaven. There is no failure for the apostle
who knows how to wait for the appointed time of Jesus, even
if it should come after his death. An old priest had sown
in trial, in tears, and also in confidence, despite great ad-

versity. He died without seeing the fruits of his labor and
prayers. A young man replaced him for whom everything
was successful. The people said, "There finally is the priest
we needed!"—quite unaware that he did nothing but reap
what the other had sown.

Another fruit of peace is equilibrium of soul. Peaceful
souls are neither pessimists nor neurotics. They are not
smug optimists, but have a wise and legitimate optimism,
based on the Heart of Jesus, for they know that nothing
happens but what God wills, and that for the man who lives
in faith, everything is grace, everything is love. Mild temper,
forbearance, goodness, serenity, only grow in peace.

Notice that it is not by keeping you away from temptations and struggles that our Lord will guard you. St. Paul
believed this when, after having been transported to the
third heaven, an angel of Satan buffeted him in order that
he might not take pride in himself, so that he prayed three
times for deliverance. But Jesus answered him, "My grace
is sufficient for you" (2 Cor 12:9). Elsewhere St. Paul cries,
"The good which I will, I do not; but the evil which I will
not, that I do. . . . Unhappy man that I am, who shall deliver me from this body of death?" (Rom 7:24). And he was
not delivered from it.

Remember that the grace of Jesus is sufficient for you,
and that it will never be lacking. It is so important to find
calmness right away again after each fall! With one look
toward him, say to him, "Jesus, one tear from your eyes,
one drop of your blood on my soul, and everything will be
purified and my soul will be in peace." "We know," says
St. Paul, "that to those who love God all things work together for good" (Rom 8:28). "Even their sins," adds St.
Augustine.

Trouble, sadness, bitterness after a sin, often come from
offended self-love. We regret less the sin as such than the
fact that it humiliates us. Peace does not necessarily mean
sensible joy. But it is the happiness of him who knows he
is where he ought to be and who asks for nothing but what

he has, who is always joyous because Jesus, who is all his joy, is always with him.

"My grace is sufficient for you." The life of grace is a beginning of the life of glory. *Gratia semen gloriae.* We begin our heaven here below in the divine peace Jesus gives us. Our only happiness on earth lies in that. The world shrinks the heart without ever filling it. Jesus makes it grow continually and fills it continually.

Besides, this peace radiates from the faces of those who are united to God, his saints. It is something calm, serene, like a beautiful lake without ripples. This inner serenity which appears externally is a true sermon, for it is a great glory for Jesus that his best servants are so tranquil, so happily peaceful under his gaze, in the radiance of his Heart.

It is a duty for you to spread this sweet and joyful peace around you, but, as little Thérèse so knowingly remarked, "not like judges of peace, but like angels of peace."[3]

Here again the Host speaks to us. The living silence of the Host preaches a heavenly peace.

Jesus expects to find it at least in the hearts of his friends, since it is the heritage which we have received from him. He finds it so seldom!

In spite of the admonitions of popes and bishops, in spite of the more or less disinterested efforts of certain heads of state, in spite of international organizations, war is everywhere. And the profound cause of this discord is the pride of nations and of men. Each one of us is partly responsible for this because of our pride. It is through the hearts of those who love him and whom he has filled with his divine peace, "choosing the weak to confound the strong" *(1 Cor 1:27),* that Jesus radiates peace in the world. The first way to work for peace in the world is to let Jesus establish it in our souls.

Chapter 6

Fraternal Charity

〰〰〰〰〰〰〰〰〰〰〰〰〰〰〰〰〰〰〰〰〰〰〰〰〰〰

Only once in the Gospel does Jesus introduce his teaching with the very strong, *"Discite a me,"* "Learn of me." What is this great, fundamental lesson?

"Learn of me because I am meek and humble of heart" *(Mt 11:29)*. Come to my school. I am the model. Following this model, what must you imitate before all else? Meekness and humility.

Meekness and humility are closely united. Meekness is the flower of humility. If you are humble, Jesus will be in you and you will radiate his own meekness to those near you.

In order to be humble, meek, and charitable, we must begin by loving Jesus. Love him, first of all, with an immense love, then read in his eyes and in his heart, what you must be for others who, after all, are not really "the others" since they are, like you, members of his Mystical Body or, at least, called to be such.

It is said that St. John, at the end of his life, repeated a single teaching continually: "Love one another!" How well can I understand him! What is not said, but of which I am sure, is that he added, obsessed by Jesus and by love, "In order to love one another, love the Lord; plunge yourselves into his heart and draw love for others out of this abyss of charity."

If there are two commandments pertaining to love, the second, the love of our neighbor, is one with the first, the love of God with our whole heart, with our whole soul, with our whole mind, and with our whole strength (cf. Mk. 12:30).

The great prayer of Jesus to his Father at the Last Supper, "that they may be one, as we also are one: I in them

and you in me," was at the same time a commandment to
love, a commandment of unspeakable importance: *Ut unum
sint (Jn 17:22)* that we might be united collectively, but first
of all, that each soul might be united with Jesus and in him
with the Father.

In order to realize this unity we need great charity in
our common life, which offers a continually renewed occasion to practice it by forgetting ourselves, and preferring
others to ourselves.

Do not start thinking, "I would like to be a hermit. I
would commit fewer sins against charity." On the contrary,
profit from life in common with others to become better—
to become holy. You are, without intending it, excellent
instruments of humiliation and mortification for each other.
Love each other, not in spite of that, but because of it.

In the same way as strength is made perfect in weakness, charity is made perfect in temptations against charity.
The occasion does not make the man, it shows what he is.
It would be easy to be patient if there were no occasion
for impatience. I have spoken to you at length about abandonment. It rests above all on obedience. It must go further;
it must go to the point of accepting, with a smile on your
lips, the pin pricks, the thorns, the contradictions which
come to you every day and very often during the day from
those near you. You have there a gold mine to exploit with
many sacrifices.

All of you have good qualities—great qualities. Are you
not the marvels of creation, made in the image of God?
All of you are masterpieces of his love, wounded, disfigured
by sin, but remade by the Redeemer, more beautiful than
before—and at what a price! You whom he has brought
together here are loved, each one of you, with a great love
of predilection.

Elevate your thoughts to that level when you look at
your brothers and sisters. Think of their souls and see especially their good qualities. Ask in your prayers to see the
beauty of the souls which surround you. A soul in a state

of grace is the dwelling place of the Father and of Jesus, the temple of the Holy Spirit. It participates in the intimate life of the three divine persons. If I could see the splendor of such a soul, I would die from the vision. Lord, increase my faith, so that, not stopping at externals but penetrating beyond them, I may know how to contemplate these divine realities.

"Lord, that I may see" *(Lk 18:41)*.

I do not love my neighbor only for the love of God, as is sometimes said. I love him for himself, and have an immense respect for him. We have a tendency to become obsessed by the faults of those around us. That is understandable: it is their faults which make us suffer and this suffering in turn reminds us of them continually. Yet do not I, myself, have even worse faults? We always come back to the case of the mote and the beam! *(cf. Lk. 6:41)* Faults are ugly. Why not look at the virtues which are beautiful? I told you that you must apply yourselves to seeing things with the eyes of Jesus, as he sees them, to loving what he loves.

What does our Lord see in our actions? The intention which motivates us. It is that which gives value to our actions. But the good intentions of others so often escape our notice. Do not judge intentions. I assure you, it has happened to me that, having ascribed a bad intention to someone, I have later had the proof, neat and clear, that I was wrong, that he had something completely different in mind than what I thought. What a lesson! As much as you can, ascribe good intentions to your neighbor. (I say "as much as you can", because at times, of course, the contrary is as plain as daylight.) Do not put final labels on others, as if no correction were possible. Shun definitive labels, especially with children. If you are tempted to prefer yourself to others, you can always think, "If so-and-so had received the graces I have received, would he not be much better than I am?"

Little Thérèse wrote, "When I want to increase in myself my love of neighbor, especially when the devil tries to put before the eyes of my soul the faults of this or that sister who is less appealing to me, I hasten to seek out her virtues, her good desires. I tell myself that if I have seen her fall one time, she may well have undergone a great many victories that she hides through humility, and that even what appears as a fault to me could very well be an act of virtue because of the intention. Ah, I understand now that perfect charity consists of enduring the faults of others, of not being at all astonished at their weaknesses, of being edified by the smallest acts of virtue which one sees them practice."[1]

Perhaps you recall having read the account she gives of her difficulties with Sister St. Peter, the good, elderly invalid whom it was necessary to lead from the choir to the refectory, which was no small affair, as she was very demanding.

"It cost me a lot," she writes, "to offer myself to render this little service, for I knew it was not easy to please her." But in order not to miss such a beautiful occasion to exercise charity, she offered herself as her guide. "It is incredible," she repeats, "how much effort that cost me!" You see that little Thérèse also had strong natural dislikes to overcome. But because of her many considerations and delicate attentions, she finally got completely into the good graces of the poor sister, especially because before leaving her she gave her most beautiful smile to her.[2]

When St. Francis de Sales refused someone something, the person left just as satisfied as if he had been granted it; for he refused with such goodness, giving his reasons and showing his regret at not being able to please. They left as content with his "no" as if they had received a "yes."

Listen to St. Paul:

"Bless those who persecute you: bless and curse not. Rejoice with those who rejoice; weep with those who weep, being of one mind one towards another, not minding high things, but consenting to the humble. Be not wise in your own conceits, to no man rendering evil for evil, providing good things, not only in the sight of God, but also in the sight of all men. If it be possible, as much as is in you, have peace with all men. . . . Be not overcome by evil, but overcome evil by good" *(Rom 12:14).*

Obviously you are not expected to experience the same feelings in your heart toward a friend and toward someone who wishes you evil. It is also clear that if your opinion is asked with a view to granting someone a position, for example, you are obliged to give an objective evaluation of him. It also might happen that the defense of truth and justice would be in question, or that the duty of fraternal correction would be imposed upon you, which is an act of charity.

There are even holy kinds of anger. But always remember that nothing troubles hearts, nothing troubles Jesus in us like dissension and discord. Nothing is more directly opposed to him. Think too of the havoc that can be wrought by speaking ill of another, or even more by detraction, because it is more difficult to set right. Be aware that a grudge nurtured voluntarily can bring about grave misunderstandings and at times can create an abyss or erect a mountain of ice between two persons. No one is completely in control of his first reactions, but you must recollect yourself very quickly. "To pardon an injustice received is to heal the wound in your own heart," said St. Vincent de Paul.

We must forget ourselves. A person who forgets himself brings joy to those around him. He quickens hearts everywhere he goes. Goodness attracts goodness—and what is more, it gives birth to goodness. It radiates something already heavenly. On the other hand, spitefulness causes sadness, closes hearts, hardens faces, brings a cold chill wherever it appears. Of course, I am speaking of a spitefulness which is voluntarily and willfully nurtured. Then the imagination starts working, a thousand phantoms invade the mind, grievances multiply, all sorts of bad intentions are taken for granted. The spiteful person starts putting facts together which in reality are totally unrelated, in order to make his neighbor's offenses seem greater, to put his neighbor in an inexcusable position in order to excuse himself. The devil fans these smouldering embers.

There are so many excuses to be found for the faults of others: their heredity, their education, their temperament, their interior trials, their physical state. Everyone, without exception, has virtues by which we can be edified. It is just and it is a joy to think about the goodness in our neighbor!

On her sick bed, surrounded with cares, little Thérèse had compassion on suffering souls: "We must treat them, even the most imperfect, with precautions like those that are taken for bodily ills. Oh, very often people do not think about that; they wound them by inattentiveness, by tactlessness, although what they need is for us to care for them and comfort them with all our power. Yes, I feel that I must have as much compassion for the spiritual infirmities of my sisters as they have for my physical infirmities."[3]

I have seen souls already advanced who have fallen because they failed to endure an injustice and exaggerated it, as I just said, and so were immersed and drowned in this backwash. One drowns very quickly in gall. Keep watch therefore, over your soul, swallow the bitterness as Jesus swallowed the vinegar on Calvary, and know how to smile at those who cause you pain. Forgive a thousand times as Jesus forgives you a hundred thousand times.

Listen to the Master: "If your brother sin against you seven times in a day, and seven times in a day he be converted unto you, saying, 'I repent,' you shall forgive him" *(Lk 17:4)*. And to Peter who asked, "Lord how often shall my brother offend against me and I forgive him? Till seven times?" Jesus answered, "I say not to you till seven times; but till seventy times seven times" *(Mt 18:21)*. Without limit.

There is also envy, which is much more widespread than

one would think, because envious people neither dare to confess their envy, nor even to admit it to themselves, their feelings seem so base to them. Envy causes much suffering, first because it grips the heart and then because it brings profound humiliation. It is believing others more favored than oneself, envying them bitterly, envying even their virtues, their piety—that is spiritual envy. I have compassion on such people who are envious in spite of themselves; but let them not forget that "by the envy of the devil, death came into the world" *(Wis 2:24)*.

It often gives rise to hatred. Following a humiliation, an injustice, a slander, resentment or bitterness are sometimes exceedingly strong. There is a real boiling inside us, a tempest in the heart. How do we calm down all of that? We must not let our will consent to it, but say with all our will, "I do not will, no, I do not approve these feelings of vengeance which are in me and which, in spite of myself, rise to attack my heart. I repudiate them."

And it is here again that we must not confuse temptation with consent. Even if the resentment is very strong, so strong that we do not succeed in dominating it, it is possible not to consent to it. It is perhaps with the fine point of my will that I will say, "I do not consent," when my whole nature in turmoil cries out the contrary. But what counts is this "no," for it depends on our will whether we say sincerely "yes" or "no"; it does not depend on our will—at least directly—whether we feel or do not feel anger. If you have not consented, you have not been lacking in charity.

How do you prove to yourself that you have not consented? Well, say to yourself, "If I meet this person who has made me suffer, for whom I feel such antipathy, will I be kind to him? Am I ready to do him a favor? To ask a favor of him (which is more difficult, for I would then owe him gratitude)? To smile at him?" Answer "yes" with all your might!

Perhaps when the times comes you will not have the cour-

age to do it. This is possible, but let your disposition of soul
and will be such that you would hope to do it. What you
always and immediately can do is to pray for that person,
trying to put your whole heart into it. Do not pray only
for his conversion—that would be irony—but that he may
receive as much good as you wished him evil in spite of
yourself.

If you thus guard your profound and habitual disposition
of soul, to make it a disposition of charity, of benevolence,
although waves of spitefulness, bitterness, rancor, hatred,
jealousy perhaps, may be rolling over you, and you think,
"How bad I am! Is it possible that I should have such feelings?" If you could only see Jesus' look of compassion, tenderness, love upon you because you are struggling, because
you have said, "I love him who has hurt me, and I shall
do my very best to show him that!"

Is that a lie? No! What misleads us is that in human
love, as it is generally viewed, it would be a lie. But truly
to love someone is sincerely to will good for him, whatever
feelings one may have at the moment.

See how important it is to make this distinction between
our nature and our will borne by grace, between what we
feel and what we will. I have already told you this, and tell
you again with regard to fraternal charity, for it is one of
the points upon which we are most tempted.

I assure you that I like a hundred times better those
sensitive natures who suffer profoundly, who feel the stings,
who react strongly, who kick, than the soft, indifferent,
passive natures from whom everything slides off without penetrating. I prefer the former, on the condition that their
reactions are occasions of victory for them, that they profit
from them to unite themselves more closely to Jesus and
to give him the proof that it is him they love, repudiating
what displeases him. The occasion for struggle is the occasion for victory. We do not have to yield deliberately,
and, with the grace of God, we can always overcome. Ask
him to rebuke the rising waves, to calm them, ask him who

in the boat stilled the furious sea with one word.

He will not calm it right away, because these very struggles which humiliate us are precious, and if it were enough to say a little prayer to become instantly an angel of meekness, it would be too easy. Often he will leave you the trial, he will leave you the humiliation, but he will help you stay united to his will in the very center of the storm. And if it has happened that you have yielded, you will pick yourself up very quickly, asking him to make everything right: "Jesus, repair what I have done badly."

A notion which is not widespread and which, nevertheless, is very important is that Jesus, when we ask him with confidence, repairs not only the evil we have done in ourselves, but also the evil we have done around us.

Indeed, he has made things right in me, but what about the evil I have done to others? The bad example I have set, the scandal I have given, the good I would have been able to do and did not do, the injustice I committed? I am set aright myself, but what about the others?

Say then, "Jesus, from this evil also which I have wrought around me, draw forth good. Even, I dare to ask you, draw a greater good from it than if I had not done the evil. I ask you this humbly, in my smallness, beating my breast and saying, *Mea culpa,* with a contrite heart, recognizing my fault. I ask it of you with an immense confidence, recognizing your mercy and the limitless price you paid for our Redemption. Make reparation in me and around me." We cannot always repair things ourselves. We cannot always ask pardon of those offended, make excuses, put things right—at least not immediately—and often the remedy would be worse than the evil. So say, "I would like to do it, I cannot, but you will do it yourself, because of my confidence."

It has been said, "For everything there is a price," and it is true. But Jesus has paid the whole price himself, first of all. He will have me pay the price with him by uniting myself with his redemptive sufferings, with his saving love, but not as a demanding and vindictive creditor. Without

him, what can I do? Nothing. With him, everything. "Come
to me, all you that labor and are burdened: and I will refresh you" *(Mt. 11:28)*. I emphasize this because I know that
this loving certainty that the Savior makes things right is
necessary to you for the peace of your souls.

I emphasize this because I know that this loving certainty
that the Savior makes things right is necessary to you for
the peace of your souls.

His Redemption is superabundant. His reparation is universal. Nothing is ever irreparable with him, and if he wills,
he can repair immediately and totally. It is a matter of faith
and hope, in humility and good will.

You must believe that he will do it. He is touched by
your bitter regret at having done wrong. He is touched
by your pain. He is touched even more by your confidence,
and that attracts even more his mercy on you. You must
live with Jesus in charity, making your life one with his
life, your King, your Friend, your Brother, who is always
there to help you in the struggle, to pick you up again
when you fall.

How marvelous it is to have with you always, Jesus who
saves you continually, who takes care of everything freely,
provided that you believe that he does it because you ask
him humbly, recognizing that you merit nothing. What about
your collaboration? You collaborate above all, once again,
by means of the theological virtues which, truly lived, require so many sacrifices, the forgetfulness of self to the
point of heroism. You see how hatred of sin, refusal to
consent to evil, humility, confidence, charity, peace all go
together as they are all only one in the infinitely merciful
Heart of Jesus.

Therefore charity is a unity: love of God and love of our
brothers are inseparable. Under the old law it was written,
"You shall love your neighbor as yourself" *(Lv 19:18)*, and
already that seemed very difficult. Yet Jesus asked more of
his apostles. He modified this precept of the Old Testament. He made a new precept of it, his own precept:

"A new commandment I give unto you: that you love one another as I have loved you" *(Jn 13:34)*. "I will that you love one another not only as each of you loves himself, I will that you love one another as I myself love you—that means without limits."

There is a very beautiful thought to consider here. It is that you can say to him, "Jesus, to love my neighbor as you love me is impossible with my poor heart so small, so narrow, so mean. Therefore, in giving me this precept, you must give me your own heart, to fulfill it." How could he resist such logic, one that must make him smile?

How strong and eloquent are the words in Holy Scripture which call us to this charity: "Judge not and you shall not be judged. Condemn not and you shall not be condemned. Forgive and you shall be forgiven" *(Lk 6:37)*. In the Our Father there are seven petitions and only a single commitment on our part: "Forgive us as we forgive." "Love your enemies," said Jesus. "And if you love those who love you, what thanks are due to you? For sinners also love those who love them. And if you do good to those who do good to you, what thanks are due to you? For sinners also do this. . . . But love your enemies: do good, and lend, hoping for nothing from it, and your reward shall be great, and you shall be sons of the Highest. For he is kind to the unthankful and the evil" *(Lk 6:27, 32, 33, 35)*. This is what distinguishes the true child of God. They will know you by the fact that you love your enemies. That will be the sign of recognition.

"Charity covers a multitude of sins" *(1 Pt 4:8)*. But a multitude of good actions does not replace charity. St. John says, "He who loves his brother abides in the light. . . . We know that we have passed from death to life, because we love the brethren. He who loves not abides in death. . . . If any man says: I love God, and hates his brother, he is a liar" *(1 Jn 2:10, 3:14, 4:20)*. What a source of peace to be assured of life because we love our brothers!

Have you meditated on the last judgment which will be

based entirely on the virtue of charity:

"For I was hungry and you gave me to eat; I was thirsty
and you gave me to drink; I was a stranger and you took
me in; naked and you covered me; sick, and you visited me;
I was in prison and you came to me. . . . As long as you
did it to one of these my least brethren you did it to me.
. . . Come, you blessed of my Father" *(Mt 24:35).*

Poverty, austerity, fasting, prayer, the gift of miracles,
without love of our brothers, all are pure illusion. To love
Jesus without loving those whom he loved unto death is not
to love him. There is no true love of neighbor without beginning by loving Jesus; but the love of Jesus is accomplished, perfected, consummated, in the love of neighbor.
"Jesus, meek and humble of heart, give me your heart to
love my neighbor."

"We are all a single body and there is no difference
among us but that which exists between one member and
the other."[4]

Every day we have the opportunity to gather around the
Eucharistic Table, in the joy of a common banquet of which
the food is the Living Bread come down from heaven.

"For we, being many, are one bread, one body: all who
partake of one bread" *(1 Cor 10:17).*

The whole liturgy revolves around this divine reality: I
pray in union with the Holy Church, my Mother, to whom
my life belongs entirely.

Because this retreat is above all a retreat on the interior
life, I have spoken to you especially about charity toward
your near neighbor, the one who gives you, doubtless, the
most to struggle against in yourself.

Have no doubt that it is in the degree to which you
change yourself that everything around you will change. A
new world will not be remade except if you become yourself this "new man," of whom St. Paul speaks, "created
according to God in justice and holiness of truth" *(Eph 4:24).*
If you are just men you will radiate justice; if you are men

of mercy, you will radiate mercy; if you are men of truth you will radiate truth; if you are men of peace, you will radiate peace. Yes, change yourself by letting Jesus transform you into himself by love.

Living in this union with him, which I have preached to you, your interior life will push you as if in spite of yourself, under the action of grace, to give yourself to others in social life, to work with all your strength for the unity of the Church, ecumenism, according to the directions of the pope and the teaching of the Council and the encyclicals.

Then, in accordance with what is possible for you, you will be led to fly to the aid of the poor, the sick, the lepers, the hungry, of all who suffer and grieve. "Let each one feel himself responsible," said Pope John XXIII, "for the realization of the common good in all sectors of social life."

You will put yourself at the disposition of your bishops and your priests, in the great family of the parish and of your chaplains, in Catholic action. Approved writings and sermons are not lacking to guide you in this important social and collective charity; and, there is no lack of associations for prayer, study, and work in common, which seek to carry out the instructions of the Holy Father.

There is a special grace attached to prayer in common. Did not Jesus say, "Where there are two or three gathered together in my name, there am I in the midst of them" *(Mt 18:20).* To be happy is to love together.

You will not think egotistically about your own perfection. Social injustices will prevent you from sleeping.

The doctrine of abandonment, which sees God in everything, will make you marvelously available for this work. This is one of its richest secrets, for it obliges us to renounce, when necessary, our own views and our little personal plans, even our plans for sanctification.

This total abandonment is the pinnacle of holiness and love, because it identifies us more perfectly with Jesus who lived only to do the will of his Father.

Chapter 7

The Apostolate

The charity of charities is the apostolate.

"I was hungry and you gave me to eat, I was thirsty and you gave me to drink" *(Mt 25:35)*. It is urgent—oh, how urgent!—to give material bread to the two men out of three in this valley of tears, who haven't enough to eat, and thus to respond to the poignant *Misereor super turbam*, *(Mk 8:2)* ("My heart goes out to the multitude") of Jesus, heartsick with compassion, as he was. But it is the "Bread of Life," the "Water which wells up unto life eternal" *(Jn 4:14)* which they need still more.

It was after "having instructed them at length," the gospel reports to us, that Jesus multipled the five loaves and two fish and distributed them to the crowd who listened to him *(cf. Mk 6:34)*. For "not by bread alone does man live, but by every word that proceeds from the mouth of God" *(Mt 4:4)*.

We must share freely with our brothers the lights, the graces which we have freely received. Paul VI affirms, "You know well that it is the task of the whole Church to continue to develop the mission of salvation of all whom Christ entrusts to her. This task belongs not only to the hierarchy, but to the laity also, by virtue of their membership in the Mystical Body of Christ, and of their participation in his mission and his royal priesthood. They have the right, the duty, and the honor—confirmed and affirmed by the sacraments of baptism and confirmation—to exercise the apostolate of the Church in the way which is proper to them."[1]

In speaking of the apostolate, I shall begin with a strong statement: in order to be fruitful apostles, begin by being saints—souls of love. The only fruitfulness is holiness. Look

at St. John Vianney, the Cure of Ars. The soul of every
apostolate is the apostle's intimate love and his immolation.

"Unless the grain of wheat falling into the ground die,
it remains alone" *(Jn 12:24)*.

"As the branch cannot bear fruit of itself, unless it abide
in the vine, so neither can you, unless you abide in me.
I am the vine: you the branches. He that abides in me,
and I in him, the same bears much fruit: for without me
you can do nothing" *(Jn 15:4)*.

Be souls of love in order to become apostles and you will
discover a very beautiful thing: that at the bank of love,
the more you give, the richer you become.

You must hear the continuous echo in your heart of the
cry of sorrowful love, of great redemptive desire, the cry
of anguish and at the same time of tenderness, the cry
of Jesus on the cross: *Sitio,* "I thirst" *(Jn 19:28)*. I thirst
for your love; you upon whom I have showered my love,
give me to drink. Treasure the spiritual riches I have given
you without limit. Find for me hearts whose love will be
like dew upon my burning lips on Calvary.

To be an apostle is to give Jesus to souls and souls to
Jesus by making him known in order to make him loved,
by filling yourself with him in order to give him, according to the beautiful definition of Father Mateo, "An apostle
is a chalice full of Jesus which overflows onto souls." Be
such chalices first of all and even before acting you will
be apostles.

Souls are on the way to perdition—what anguish! Think
of these souls for whom the Savior has suffered so much,
has poured out all his blood. Such souls, made for happiness, risk being lost forever in hell, being fixed, like Satan,
in the hatred of him who is nothing but love, banished forever to the place on whose gate Dante wrote, "All hope
abandon, you who enter here." Remember that a place
exists where a soul can no longer say, "Jesus, I have confidence in you; save me."

In Gethsemane, Jesus saw in a vision the price of souls.

And he trembled—he, the divine strength: "Father, if you will, remove this chalice from me: but yet not my will, but yours be done" *(Lk 22:41)*. And a sweat of blood flowed from him onto the earth, under the pressure of the agony which bore down upon him as he faced the consequences of sin.

It depends upon us whether more or fewer are saved. The field of the apostolate is immense: there are so many who have been led astray by impurity, by the pride which leads to hatred. Think of the ignorance, the indifference of the masses who are without Christ, either in life or death—these multitudes without God. Think of the millions of pagans who cover the world in greater numbers each day, sheep outside the fold. Imagine the many baptized who lack a supernatural outlook—that too is a sorrow—who lack confident love and the apostolic flame, who call themselves the friends of Jesus yet are his friends so little.

I thirst! Love is not loved. "Love and cause to be loved the love which is not loved." There, surely, is the most beautiful cry which could come from the lips of an apostle. It came from the heart of St. Francis of Assisi: "Love and cause to be loved the love which is not loved."

But you know, before the apostolate of word and action, there is the apostolate of prayer and suffering, without which the external apostolate would be nothing, nothing at all. Words and actions come only in the last place, after what I call the apostolate of silence in love, which was the great apostolate of Jesus and Mary at Nazareth for thirty years.

Jesus did not preach in that silence except by what he was: the incarnate Word of God. You also preach by what you are: children of God, confirmed in the Holy Spirit and sharing the divine life through the Eucharist. He preached by his example; you also preach by your example, if you are the Christians you ought to be.

I have often meditated upon this scene in the Gospel: Jesus comes back to Nazareth which he had left shortly

before. He enters the synagogue, arises to read, unrolls
the book of the prophet Isaias and begins to expound it.
His numerous hearers, struck with astonishment, say,

"Is not this the son of Joseph? How came this man by
this wisdom and miracles? Is not this the carpenter's son?
Is not his mother called Mary, and his brethren James
and Joseph and Simon and Jude? . . . And they were scan-
dalized in his regard" *(Cf. Lk 4:16-29, Mt 13:54 ff).*

Now those who were listening to him were Nazarenes, his
daily companions, his childhood friends.

There is a lesson to be taken from this scene. We must
conclude from it that for thirty years Jesus did not make
a single gesture, did not say a single word which could
have revealed who he was. He remained so hidden and
silent that for all those who had lived with him, the friends
of Mary and Joseph and his own friends, he was the carpenter, the son of Joseph, and that was all.

We find only five or six references in the Gospel to Mary,
Queen of the Apostles. It is certain that she instructed the
apostles, although it is not revealed to us.

Concerning St. Joseph, patron of the universal Church,
there is complete silence. It is not even known where he
was buried. Where is his tomb? He has disappeared totally.

What fruitfulness there is in self-effacement, intimate
prayer, immolation, silence! It is this that I call "the secret of
Nazareth." Father Charles de Foucauld understood it well.

We must immolate ourselves, we must die to ourselves
in order to preach. There is no truly radiant preacher who
has not lived the *quotidie morior,* 'I die daily,' of St. Paul
(1 Cor 15:31).

The desert fathers reproduced the immolation and the
silence of Nazareth and thus revivified the newly born
Church.

There is no doubt that little Bernadette of Lourdes served
the Blessed Virgin much better by retiring to a convent than
if she had continued to receive visitors or if she had given

conferences on her visions.

Some time ago I visited the motherhouse of the Little Sisters of the Poor in the diocese of Rennes. The good mother superior led me to the cemetery. There in the center was a magnificent tomb with a beautiful cross of sculptured stone. Instinctively I said to her, "This is doubtless the tomb of Jeanne Jugan, your foundress?" "No," she answered, "it is that of our second superior general. Jeanne Jugan began the work at St. Servan, by receiving into her home first one poor old woman, then a second. Wishing to give aid to still others, she sought companions to help her." That is how this admirable foundation of the Little Sisters of the Poor was born.

Certain events which God permitted—without directly willing them—as he does to test his saints, resulted in the nomination of another religious as superior general. Jeanne Jugan again took up her little basket to go out and beg for her dear old people. She returned to the ranks, as they say, completely effaced. It was known afterwards how much she suffered from this interiorly, but she uttered not a single word of complaint, "And she died forgotten by men."[2]

The mother superior added, "Today, if we wish to receive favors, if we wish to obtain miracles, it is not the beautiful stone tomb to which we must go to pray, it is to the little tomb of Jeanne." A little tomb which lay there, lost among the others, with its wooden cross planted in the earth. Since then they have exhumed her and transported her into the chapel of the motherhouse. But when I was there, not too long ago, she was still where she had been since 1879, the year of her death.

I am certain that Jeanne Jugan did more for the foundation of the Little Sisters of the Poor by this humble acceptance of being cast.aside and by her self-effacement than by any other works which she might have accomplished. Such is the seed which is buried in order to bear fruit. Here we are in the midst of full divine reality.

Little Saint Thérèse lived a life of silence and immola-

tion for nine years. Shortly before her death, as she rested
in her cell during the recreation time, she heard one sister
in the kitchen remarking, "My sister Thérèse of the Child
Jesus will die soon, and I really wonder what our mother
will be able to say about her after her death. She will certainly be at a loss, for this little sister, lovable as she is,
has certainly done nothing which is worth the trouble to
recount."[3] Even her own sisters distributed her robes, her
linen (they were subsequently taken back in order to make
relics of them) so ordinary and hidden was her life: nothing
extraordinary on the outside, everything extraordinary on
the inside. One could apply to her, in a lesser degree, what
was said of Mary: *"Omnis gloria ejus ab intus."* All her
glory was within.

Now she is patroness of missions, on a level with St.
Francis Xavier who went to preach to the ends of the earth.
She is secondary patroness of France, along with St. Joan
of Arc, whose active public apostolate was so remarkable.[4]
I would like to tell you the story of the choice of little
Thérèse as patroness of missions. It is very interesting.

It came about through the personal initiative of Pope
Pius XI. In fact, the two Roman congregations to which
the petition of 226 missionary bishops was presented, asking
for this patronage, did not produce a favorable vote. The
majority of the members were put off, no doubt, by such
an apparent contradiction: for a little Carmelite who never
left her cloister to be put on a level with St. Francis Xavier!
But Cardinal Vico, completely won over in favor of granting this new privilege, then referred the matter to the Pope.
Pius XI departed, for once, from the custom which leaves
the solution of such cases to the Roman congregations, while
the Holy Father usually contents himself with authoritatively
ratifying the decisions which have been made by them. He
took charge personally of the promulgation of the Decree
of December 14, 1927, when St. Thérèse of the Child Jesus
was made "principal patroness, equal with St. Francis Xavier, of all missionaries, men and women, and also of all

existing missions in the entire world."[5] The Holy Father, Vicar of Christ on earth, inspired by the Holy Spirit, had perceived the will of God.

It is evident that heaven wished to give everyone a great lesson of the fruitfulness of hidden immolation, of contemplation, of the immense desire to save souls, through her, who wanted to be the love in the heart of the Church, her Mother.

The extraordinary diffusion which the cult of the Heart of Jesus acquired three centuries ago is due, in great part, to St. Margaret Mary. How did she bring it about? She immolated herself in the seclusion of the cloister, consumed by love.

St. Teresa of Avila, observing the group of virgins who surrounded her, cried magnificently, "What shall I do with them? Ah, I shall employ them to destroy heresy, to bring forth doctors of the Church, to make reparation for sins, to convert souls. They will be solid walls, armed ramparts. They will be living fountains of light and faith." — A few women, spending their whole life in the enclosure, behind four walls!

When St. Paul suffered shipwreck at Malta, he assured the others that no one would perish, because he was not going to perish. An angel had told him, "God will grant you the life of all those who voyage with you" *(Acts 27:24)*. Because of one saint, all were saved.

What is the center and source of the life of the Church? The Host in the tabernacle, the little, silent Host, the praying Host, the loving Host. The apostles preach, but from the tabernacles of the world come forth rays of divine light, parts of the sun of Love, which touch and enlighten souls. Be praying and loving hosts and you will send forth rays like the Host, and God will give you all those who "voyage" with you, your neighbors, all those whom you love and whose salvation you ardently desire.

Bearing in mind the magnificent dogma of the Communion of Saints, you must never doubt that you are really apostles, if you love, and only because you love. Jesus can hide it from you in order to increase the merit of your faith, but never doubt it. Thank him every day for the souls which you save, without knowing it, by your acts of love.

As I have already told you, it is beautiful to pray in this way: instead of saying to Jesus, "Give me souls," say to him, "I thank you for the souls which you give me simply because I am sure that you give them to me," relying on his own words: "All things, whatsoever you ask when you pray, believe that you have already received them, and they shall come unto you" *(Mk 11:24).*

Know how to unite yourself with the miracles he works in you continually, even when you do not realize and are not aware of it. "Jesus, I unite myself to the wonders you work in me. I know for certain that I love you today more than yesterday and that tomorrow I shall love you more than today, because I have opened my heart to your grace which is a torrent which ceaselessly engulfs me and continually transforms me into yourself and spreads out to others."

St. Paul tells us:

"Hope does not confound: because the charity of God is poured forth in our hearts, by the Holy Spirit who is given to us" *(Rom 5:5).*

You thus oblige Jesus to do the thing for which you thank him. Is that presumption? No, since hope does not deceive and he has promised great fruitfulness to those who have confidence.

During the visitation, so St. Luke tells us, Elizabeth addressed Mary in a great cry, "Blessed is she who has believed!" And Mary answered, *Magnificat anima mea Dominum,* "My soul magnifies the Lord" *(Lk 1:45).*

Carry a great apostolic spirit into your prayers. Pray to obtain mercy for souls. Jesus could have saved men without us. He did not will to do it that way.

"The Creator of the Universe," writes little Therese, "listens to the prayer of a very little soul to save others who are ransomed, as she is, by the price of all his blood."[6]

Some are astonished when they see the number of unbelievers, the number of pagans, of impious and impenitent
sinners in the world, compared to that of the faithful. There
is a surprising disproportion there which is hard to explain.
One might wonder whether the Redemption has not failed
after all.

I think Divine Providence has permitted this (I purposely
say permitted and not willed) in order that fervent souls
may live the apostolic spirit in a better way, with a greater
desire to save unfaithful souls, seeing how many there are,
and that they may share even more the *Sitio* ("I thirst")
of Jesus on the Cross and his *Misereor super turbam,*
("My heart goes out to the multitude"). And then because
his chosen souls, his privileged, his elect, will love him with
a greater love, Jesus himself will have mercy on others.
You see your responsibility!

He told St. Margaret Mary, "A soul which loves can obtain pardon for a thousand criminals."[7]

Pius XII in *Mystici Corporis Christi* writes: "If the
Church herself shows evident traces of our human weakness, we must attribute it not to her constitution, but rather
to the lamentable tendency toward evil which her divine
Founder has to suffer even among the most elevated members of his Mystical Body, in order to test the virtue of his
sheep and shepherds and make them increase in all the merits of Christian faith."

Do not conclude from this that the less visibly powerful the Church is on earth, the more she will fill her role
of leaven among the masses, that institutions do not have
to become Christian, that we must accept the fact that the
world is going its own way more and more without the
Church. John XXIII gave us a completely different instruc-
tion when he asked us to work to the end "that human
society may show forth with the most perfect fidelity the
image of the Kingdom of God."[8]

Also do not ask only for the return of sinners, but that
good people will become very good, and that the very good

will become saints. Do not ask only for the conversion of
souls, but for the perfection of souls, because Jesus not
only thirsts to see sinners convert, but perhaps he thirsts
even more to see the souls which he has chosen rise higher
and grow in love, and unite themselves more intimately
with him.

He needs truly loving souls, true hosts, truly transformed
into him by love. He needs such souls in order to save men.

Be assured that I have thought much about this during
this retreat, while praying for you: "Jesus, make them grow,
bring them even closer to you, that they may become united
with you, a single flame with you who, 'came to bring fire
on the earth' *(Lk 12:49)* the fire which you are yourself."

You see, the world seems to run to its destruction: yet I
am not a pessimist.

Why? Because I think that today there are more souls
than ever in cloisters and also in the world, entirely given
to Jesus in complete confidence and total abandonment, without anything which distinguishes them from others, hidden
like the Nazarene.

Evil displays itself; good remains unknown. Believe my experience on this point. These hidden souls console him, they
make reparation, they repay him and oblige him, I dare to
say, to be merciful.

These souls are sometimes called lightning rods, but I
do not like this image, for it is not thunder and lightning
which Jesus lets fall from his heart onto the world *(Lk 9:54)*,
but torrents of graces. He needs hearts which will be chan-
nels for these rushing waters, to receive them and share
them. That is the role of these faithful and generous souls.
By their very existence they hold back or destroy the consequences of sin.

Why did Mary remain on earth after the Ascension before going to be reunited with her Son in heaven? I think
it was in order to instruct the disciples, but also, and above
all, to carry on the apostolate of silence in prayer, suffering, and love. While the apostles ran in pursuit of souls,

Mary prayed near the Host which the Mass of St. John left her. And when there were already many Christians, many victim souls, praying and loving for this hidden apostolate, then Mary was able to leave. Her role was continued—with much less perfection, of course, but with the same mission on the part of the victim souls who offered themselves up, with Mary in their hearts.

We preachers realize so clearly that we are "tinkling cymbals" *(1 Cor 13:1)* if we have not love: we need to have love in our own hearts, and we need to be supported by the love of souls given over to love. I assure you that in saying this I am thinking about those who have promised to help me, to pray for the *adveniat,* who offer their sufferings and prayers for my apostolate, and it is to them that I attribute the good I am able to do.

You know that the prayer of prayers is the Mass: perfect adoration, perfect expiation, perfect thanksgiving, it is also perfect supplication of the immolated Jesus: it is the dearest treasure of the apostolate.

How much unhappiness there is in our perverted world, in the midst of the disorders caused by lack of religion, the current moral standards, divorce. How many husbands and wives, mothers of families, have come and sought me out because their spouses or their sons or daughters no longer practice the faith. "Father, what anguish! What grief! All my efforts to lead them back to God are in vain. What shall I do?" And I always answer, "First of all, pay the ransom by your Masses and your Communions, adding to the blood of Jesus in the chalice, the blood of your souls which is your tears. Then keep your confidence in the infinite mercy of the Savior. Say, like one mother I know who was distressed by the conduct of her children, 'Jesus, you love them too much not to save them.' Thank him in advance for the heaven which he is preparing for them because of your prayer, but—and this is very, very important—while you are suffering, wait in peace for the time of Jesus, the time chosen by him to grant your request. He will perhaps make you wait a long time, precisely as a proof of your confidence. Do not disappoint him; tell him, whatever your trial, that with his grace nothing will make you lose your profound peace, because you are sure of him.

Add your sufferings to the apostolate of your prayers united to the prayer of Jesus which is the Mass. He willed to save the world by suffering. In order to redeem souls with the Savior, you must suffer with him and like him. Your Mass, which is a memorial of Calvary, will be of much more value if you are there at the foot of the cross, or better still, on the cross.

These are the great riches of those who suffer, those who weep. Oh, if one could only see the very special look of tenderness which Jesus gives the poor and suffering! They have the greatest power to touch his heart and to obtain the graces they desire.

Tell this to the sick. It will always do them great good. Tell them, "Jesus looks at you with more love than the others, because you suffer. Offer your sickness to save souls. He will listen to you because you are nailed to your bed, a little as he was on his cross. He will listen to you, because he is moved with compassion for you.'

I often tell this to the sick people whom I go to visit. "I come to collect from you because you are rich in the supernatural order. You amass by your accepted trial a great capital of graces, first of all for yourself, but also for others. I come to see my capitalist." That makes them smile and gives them much courage. They are touched to see that someone considers them rich, for the idea never crossed their minds.

Ah! If only this gospel could be preached in an effective way, the social question would be solved. This does not mean that we must not look for all possible means to relieve those who suffer, to better the lot of those in trouble, to help the destitute. With what great tenderness we must bend over them, making ourselves like St. Paul, "all things to all men, weak with the weak" *(1 Cor 9:22)*, as the Holy

Church and her saints have done for centuries.

You will never be able to give too much devotion, while being indifferent to your own fatigue; to give too much of yourself, entirely forgetting yourself; to give too much of your goods to those who have none, always concerned to be the servant of those who serve you—of those workers who, at the price of their arduous toil and sweat, assure you a well-being and comfort which you do not deserve.

Drive out pitilessly the instinctive feeling of superiority which blinds those who are in a dominant position here below and who forget that many of these poor, who are their brothers, are very often much superior to them in the spiritual and supernatural order.

Thus, you must not bluntly tell someone who is not a saint and who trembles under the weight of a trial, perhaps an old man bent by age and physical deficiencies, "You have only to abandon yourself to the will of God, and you will have a more beautiful heaven one day." That could appear to be patronizing and a way of shrugging off their complaints.

However, you must always bear in mind that little by little, with a thousand light touches of tact, that is the point at which you must arrive. People do not dare speak of heaven any more, especially since the diabolically inspired Marxists have called it "the opium of the people," good only for putting the unhappy to sleep and burying their rights by the beautiful promise of a hereafter from which no one has ever come back, as they say. Yet we hardly see a hint of the paradise which they promise on earth. And where do we find the "new man" announced by Lenin?

People no longer dare to speak of heaven, yet nothing can be explained here below without this blessed place where all injustices—and God knows they exist in this world—will be put right, where the last shall be first in endless beatitude, where Jesus, ascended after his resurrection, has himself prepared a place for us, where God awaits us—God who is nothing but Love.

Who can tell the value of a suffering, of a contradiction, of a humiliation, accepted not only with resignation (I do not like this word which seems to say that one accepts because he cannot do otherwise), but accepted with joy by the will. A *Magnificat* sung on the cross, a smile in the midst of tears—what richness!

When you suffer like this, tell Jesus in total abandonment, "If by lifting my little finger I could change my situation and be relieved immediately, I would not lift my little finger, because it is you who have chosen this for me. You are wiser than I; you love me more than I love myself; I will let you do it. All is well."

This is the prayer, I know, of many sick people at Lourdes: "Lord, if you will it, you can heal me, but let your will be done before anything else." And often they ask for others to be healed before themselves if it is the plan of the divine Savior.

Pope John XXIII, in a discourse addressed to the entire world "undertook to affirm, once more, the preeminence of a total consecration to the life of prayer, above all other forms of the apostolate."[9]

Having well understood this, let us go on to speak of the apostolate of word and action.

Fides ex auditu: "faith then comes by hearing: and hearing by the word of Christ" *(Rom 10:17).*

St. Thomas says that if the active life does not harm the contemplative life, it is more perfect to unite the two, since light is made not only to shine, but to shine and illuminate. It is in part due to our weakness that the purely contemplative life is actually more perfect.

It is so beautiful to lead others to contemplate what we have contemplated, and we find new themes of contemplation in action, in contact with others.

Have I placed too much emphasis on the hidden apostolate of prayer and immolation, at this time when the Council reminds us, and rightly so, of the importance of the visible apostolate and the missions? I do not think so.

If you live this doctrine of total abandonment, of union with Jesus in faith, hope, and charity as I have presented it to you, not only will you be available for all the activities which will be asked of you or proposed to you, but in your hearts a flame will rise up, a wind, if you will—the Holy Spirit—which will push you, as if in spite of yourself, to give yourself unreservedly to your neighbor. *Caritas Christi urget nos*—"The charity of Christ impels us" *(2 Cor 5:14)*. There is no danger of inertia when you love. When everything is done in love, everything becomes prayer, contemplation.

The active apostolate of the laity is not an optional thing, a luxury, but an obligation, an imperious necessity.

When you think of the poor who die of hunger, of the victims of catastrophes, and of murderous wars, your heart breaks, your pocket-book opens. And still more your heart must break when you think that souls are dying by the millions of spiritual hunger. Jesus thirsts for these souls. They cannot go to him for they do not know him. He cannot go visibly to them, because he has condemned himself to silence, hidden in the Tabernacle. He himself needs others, because he wishes to use them as his instruments. He instituted the priesthood with a view to the Eucharistic Sacrifice; but also in order to be able to use the feet of his priests to run after strayed lambs, to use their hands to dress wounds and to bless, their lips to speak the words of truth, consolation, and salvation.

You are "a chosen generation, a kingly priesthood, a holy nation, a purchased people" *(1 Pt 2:9)*, who are baptized, and you participate in the divine priesthood by offering the Sacrifice of the Mass with the priest, but you must also participate in it by your apostolic action.

Listen to your bishops, follow their directives, enter into their pastoral works. So many diverse fields of activity are open today to those who want to be apostles!

In the ever-shifting domain of opinions and free options,

the Christian often finds himself torn. For it is not always easy to defend truth and justice—and they need defending— while preserving respect and love of neighbor. Pray with gentleness and humility, calm the passions, ask for light. You will be judged by God on the purity of your intentions. Take great care in your doctrinal formation, which is more necessary now than ever before.

We must stand with the bishops and the pope. Pius XI said, "Your bishop and the pope, are the golden chain which connect you to the Divine Redeemer. You must be with the pope, because whoever is with him is with the very foundation of the Church; for it is against him, and the Church founded on him, that the gates of hell shall not prevail."[10]

Peter is the blessed rock (which truth we know with the certainty of absolute faith), the unique source of assurance and peace, against which Satan will do battle in vain until the end of time: Peter, "the Sweet Christ on earth";[11] Peter, to whom Jesus said, turning toward him at the Last Supper,

"I have prayed for you, that your faith fail not *(Lk 22:32);* Peter, "who loves more than the others" *(cf. Jn 21:15)* and confirms them in faith and love.

Make careful distinctions with sure guides, and follow the guidelines of the Council on the liturgy, on the importance given to communal prayer and working together in the apostolate. With an ardent desire for the unity of the Church, enter into dialogue with our separated brethren in a disposition of greatest benevolence and affection which will attract reciprocity, and of which Paul VI has given us such a good example. Take upon your shoulders and into your hearts the burden of the missions. Have a missionary spirit like little Thérèse.

Listen to her words: "A single mission would not be enough for me. I would like at the same time to announce the gospel on the five continents and unto the most remote islands. I would like to be a missionary, not only for a few years, but I would like to have been one from the creation of the world until the end of time."[12]

Give yourself, without counting the cost, in an immense love for the Holy Church, born of the Blood and the Water flowing from the wound in the Heart of Jesus. She is our Mother, "pillar and ground of the truth" *(1 Tm 3:15)*, so beautiful throughout the twenty centuries which have gone by since her birth, in spite of her dark hours and her human wounds. She can only become more and more beautiful until the final victory of her Head who himself said, "I have overcome the world." He gave us this word as the source of our confidence: *Sed confidite, ego vinci mundum:* "But have confidence; I have overcome the world" *(Jn 16:33)*.

You will find unsuspected joys in this active apostolate where you will not notice your pain, where you will not heed your fatigue and repugnance, where you will have forgotten yourselves. It will be a gain for you, a fruitful experience, to adapt yourself to various situations, to various feelings, to the joys and pains of others.

What is more, you will have the happiness of speaking about Jesus, of opening hearts with this blessed name which is the key to divine power. Do not be afraid to pronounce and to repeat often the name of Jesus.

It is not a matter of indifference whether you always say, "the Lord," "Christ," or "Jesus." There is a very special grace attached to the name of Jesus. The evangelists use the name "Jesus" and St. John calls Mary *Mater Jesu*— "Mother of Jesus." Remember that it is his Father who gave him this name and who revealed it to Mary by the angel Gabriel *(cf. Lk. 1:31)*.

You will taste the joy of having spread joy, of having poured out on a wound the healing balm of the heart of Jesus, of having brought forth a smile by giving someone confidence, of having commiserated, of having given peace and made your faith and love pass into the souls of others. If you know how to open hearts in this way you will see hidden marvels, things which are confounding. You will

see that there are actually few truly bad people, but many
who are ignorant and weak. You will then know how to
keep a just mean between pessimism which is a lack of
faith, and facile optimism which does not see evil, danger,
or unleashed hell. Then how happy you will be in heaven
for having spent yourself to gain souls who will be there
also for all eternity, thanks to you!

Remember that each soul won wins others, and that you
will be forever the spiritual fathers and mothers of a multitude of elect who will come to seek you out upon your
arrival at the door of paradise, or whom you will receive
when they arrive. This heaven of which little Thérèse says,
"that we will not meet indifferent looks there because all
the elect will recognize that they are indebted among themselves to one another for the graces which shall have merited the crown for them. As a mother is proud of her children, so shall we be proud of one another, without the least
jealousy."[13] This is an entrancing scene, and no good theo-
logian will deny the truth of it.

Finally, I insist, hold fast, always with the same tena-
city, hold fast to an immense confidence, in your apostolate.
Often our Lord hides from the apostle the fruit of his work,
of his fatigue, in order to keep him humble and to test his
faith, by a wholly divine wisdom. Learn how to say, "I do
not expect my reward here below." Even if you do not see
the result of your prayers, of your supplications, of your
efforts, believe, believe!

Nothing is irreparable for Jesus and for Mary. A widow,
desperate because her husband had committed suicide by
throwing himself into a river, came to Ars and met the
Curé upon leaving the church. He bent toward her and told
her, "He is saved." As she made a gesture of incredulity,
the saint repeated emphatically, "I tell you that he is saved.
He is in purgatory and you must pray for him. Between
the parapet of the bridge and the water he had time to
make an act of repentance. It is the Blessed Virgin who obtained this grace for him. Remember the shrine to Mary

in your room? Sometimes your husband, although irreligious, united himself to your prayer. That merited repentance and the supreme pardon for him."

Before leaving, she confided to M. Guillaumet, superior of the College of St. Dizier, a witness to the scene, "I was in a dreadful state of despair imagining the tragic end of my husband. He was an unbeliever and I lived only for the thought of leading him back to God. Then he drowned himself by a voluntary suicide! I could only believe he was damned—Oh! never to see him again!—Yet you heard what the Curé of Ars told me repeatedly: 'He is saved!' I shall see him again in heaven after all!"[14]

See the delicacy of Jesus and the Blessed Virgin! A person did some good which he had forgotten, but they had not forgotten, and at the right moment they made use of it, if I may put it that way. Jesus makes use of everything to save us. How astonished we will be in heaven when we see that! Some make him a judge who strikes men down and seeks revenge, whereas in fact he seeks to save us by all possible means.

Chapter 8

The Cross

You must realize that throughout your life, at each step, you will find the cross of your divine model, your King, crucified and crowned with thorns, Jesus. Humiliation is a bitter cross. Abandonment is a real crucifixion when it is rightly understood. Mass and Communion are inseparable from Calvary. There is no reparation without penance and sacrifice. In the apostolate, the money to buy souls is suffering, accepted with love. Suppress the cross in your life, and everything crumbles. The cross is the structure. As it bore the Savior, it bears salvation, and so it must bear us also, and all our works.

I know without asking that all of you here have suffered, and you will suffer again. I am sure I will be giving you great comfort in speaking to you about the price of the cross.

Never look at the cross without Jesus. If I must bear the cross all alone, I renounce it in advance. I do not want to touch the onerous burden with the end of my finger: I am too weak, too cowardly, too sensitive. It is too hard to suffer. I deserve a hundred times to suffer without you, Jesus, but it is with you that I want to suffer. With you, I accept all the crosses, all of them—if you will bear them with me. You can hide yourself, you can make it look as though you are not there, as if I am bearing it all alone, I accept that on one condition: that you hide yourself in my heart.

How can we be Christians, the subjects of a King crowned with thorns, baptized in his blood, absolved so often by his blood, receiving Communion every day at Mass, at his Sacrifice, and yet run away from the cross? That would be to forget that the cross is a marvelous invention of divine mercy which gives us the occasion to prove to Jesus that we love him. What is a love that does not prove itself? I told you that love is a choice. What merit is there in choosing Jesus if we only have to follow him on a path of roses? How would we know whether it was he or the roses on the pathway which we were following? He wants to be loved for himself, not for his gifts. He does not want the experience of the rich who lose their friends when they lose their money and can no longer give presents.

He is jealous of our true love. Without the cross there would be many more faithful in the world; but would these be loving souls? For all eternity he wants to be able to thank us for having chosen him, in sacrifice, for having shared his cross with him. When he gives us something to suffer, said little Thérèse, it is because he wants a gift from us. What gift? A smile on the cross. He begs for our love, proven by suffering, in order to be able to say, "It is you who remained with me in the trial." How sweet it will be when we hear, for all eternity, these words from the lips of Jesus, or rather from the depths of his heart: "And you are they who have continued with me in my temptations: and I dispose to you, as my Father has disposed to me, a kingdom, that you may eat and drink at my table, in my kingdom" *(Lk 22:28)*. At his table! In his kingdom!

Another reason to love the cross is that it was the lot of your Savior, and therefore you choose it as your own lot. Must we not find good what he chose for himself, and for his Mother? Can we desire that he choose something else for us? He does not want us to consider as an evil the means by which he saved us. Do two people love one another if one regards with horror what the other regards with love? When people love one another, they have the same tastes—and Jesus wants us to share with him his taste for the cross. When two persons love each other, they desire to resemble each other.

St. Paul said, "But we preach Christ crucified" *(1 Cor 1:23)*. St. Andrew, looking at the cross to which he was to be nailed, cried, "Dear cross, welcome! Good cross which is going to permit me to die like my beloved Master." St. Francis of Assisi was inflamed by love of the cross to the point of being counted worthy to carry in his body the stigmata of our Lord. St. Teresa of Avila cried, "Either to suffer or to die." St. Margaret Mary was in love with her abjection. Little St. Thérèse hid the wounds of her crucifix under roses and hid in the same way, we might say, her own interior trials under the roses of her smiles, and discovered "the hidden treasures of the Holy Face."[1]

Moreover, suffering helps us to detach ourselves from earth, to look higher, to remember that earth is a place of passage. That is why we so often find that the poor, the suffering are much nearer to our Lord than others. Sorrow lifts us up, sorrow makes us grow, sorrow liberates. It has been said that in affluent areas where people live in great comfort they very quickly become materialistic, egotistical, indifferent. They have, so to speak, their reward on earth. On the contrary, those who suffer, provided they do not rebel against it, look toward heaven and think about eternity.

A great cross is, very often, the prelude to a great grace, even for an unbeliever. Suffering ripens the soul, sometimes very quickly. A great trial can, with one stroke, detach a soul from all that is created; it can be the source of a total conversion.

God has provided us marvelous joys on this earth. It would be ungrateful to forget them. So many beauties, which are reflections of his beauty, elevate us toward him, when they do not draw us away from him. But here below, not a single beauty is perfect, and they must always make us think of the homeland of unblemished happiness, as the beautiful "Poem of Hope" of Marietta Martin expresses it:

"One day there will be no more unexpressed words of love,
There will be no more stifled desires,
There will be no more silent presences: all the
   voices will be heard,
The veil which the music lifts will never
   more be lowered,
There will be no more inaccessible space, and the
   spool of time will unwind in the present,

All the sister particles of souls will join together.
The sunsets will be explained,
Beauty will lose its anguish,
Creation will be the clear word of divinity,
One day, like a beautiful voyage toward the beloved dead."

All Love's chosen ones are given trials. When I find that a soul is very closely united to Jesus, very intimate with him, I do not need to ask, "Have you suffered in your life? Have you had trials, crosses, bitternesses?" I am sure that he has passed by the road of Calvary to arrive at this union with the Crucified.

Therefore the cross is a means for Jesus to lead back to himself those who do not love him, to bring closer those who do not love him enough, and to consummate in himself those who do love him.

Suffering is an expiation of sin. Jesus willed to wash our crimes in his blood but, in order to participate in this sorrowful Redemption, we must know also how to be, at least in part, "a man of sorrows." It is an inescapable law; we must pass that way. You see, we cannot expiate sin, which is a guilty pleasure, except by suffering. Penance, penance— the holy books are filled with this word. The Blessed Virgin reminded us of it at Lourdes, at La Salette, and at Fatima.

In order to enter into a country as marvelous as heaven, to appear before the God of infinite purity and beauty, to see him face to face, to participate in the divine nature, to take part in the intimate life of the Holy Trinity—since that is our sublime predestination—in order to know God as he knows himself, to love him as he loves himself, we must be purified like gold in the crucible; we must have the wedding garment, washed in the blood of the Lamb, but washed also in the blood of our souls, which is our tears.

But, and I insist on this "but," do not ever stop at the isolated idea of expiation by the cross, without going further. Whether or not you are given the cross in order to expiate, the cross is always given in love. It is always presented by

Jesus in a design of love. It is always an occasion to prove our love and, if you take it that way, it will then acquire the greatest value of expiation. Therefore, with all your crosses you can say, "Lord, I accept it especially as a proof of your love for me." That is the point to which your faith must go: to see the love of Jesus in all your crosses.

We always see the cross as reparation, but not enough as preparation. It is a preparation for the graces which Jesus wants to give us, which he wants to shower upon us; it is a gift he gives us: "Do you will to accept a thorn from my own crown, stained with my blood? Do you will to accept a particle of my cross? It is in love that I offer it to you, it is in love that I give it to you, it is in love that I impose it upon you. If you accept, with joy, this gift of my wounded heart, you permit me to shower my graces upon you."

I am insistent upon this point because it is an unfashionable notion. We often accept the cross very generously, saying, "I certainly deserved it." We see it as a just chastisement, a consequence of our infidelities. Rising a bit higher, we accept it as an expiation of our faults. Rarely do we rise to the point of seeing in it Jesus' attentiveness, his gentleness, a proof of his tenderness. Yet it is always that.

Tell me, is it not true that your first thought when you are sorely tried, perhaps after the first natural reaction of revolt, is to accept your cross with a bent back, as a just consequence of your sins, and leave it at that? This is right in part, but it is not believing enough in Love. It is the response of a slave, not of a friend.

Moreover, the cross is a priceless means for the saving of souls. I have already spoken to you about the apostolate of suffering. In his delicacy, Jesus does not will to save souls without associating us with his saving action, and it is by the cross that they are redeemed. When we are suffering greatly, how weak we seem to ourselves under the burden of pain. It is a source of great strength to say to Jesus,

"I am suffering and I am happy to suffer because it is a gift of your love; but in exchange, give me souls. I am sure that you give me the souls of those I love who do not love you." This gives us great courage to suffer: not only to say to him, "Give them to me," but, "I am sure that you give them to me in exchange for these sufferings. I join with you in paying the ransom, advancing the money. Jesus, you will not be outdone in generosity." Think of all those for whom you purchase eternal bliss by a suffering which is, after all, transitory. Suffering is a gold mine to exploit for saving souls, for helping missionaries, for being a hidden apostle. What happiness it is to be able to suffer when we cannot act!

It is impossible to fulfill our Christian mission on earth without suffering. It seems that the greater the missions are, the more the crosses are too, and the heavier they are. The crosses of parents, the crosses of apostles, the crosses of priests, the crosses of bishops, the crosses of the pope. The Lord has given us a field to work, and we must irrigate it with tears falling from the wine press of sorrow, in order that it may be fruitful.

How many eloquent reasons there are to love the cross, yet how we forget them in the current of life! In our days, how many plans we make, little calculations—very often unconscious, I must say—which are made simply to avoid suffering! We flee it in the first movement of our nature which finds it so repugnant and we must not be astonished by that. We surprise ourselves: "Wait; I have made this little plan. Why? Fundamentally, it was to avoid an annoyance, a humiliation." Do not be angry with yourself because of this first instinctive movement of nature. If it did not rear up, that would mean that it entailed no suffering. Our nature's first reflexes are to avoid whatever threatens harm.

Therefore, do not be surprised at this, but be in the state of soul, the disposition (I always come back to this) where you can say to Jesus, "I do not fear any cross because I know that when a cross comes you always come too." The

Crucified is never found without the cross and neither is the cross found without the Crucified. It always bears Jesus. I press it to my breast to press him at the same time to my heart. So tell him, "With you I do not fear any cross."

Note that this is not to ask for the cross. Little Thérèse, a few weeks before her death, said, "Oh, I would never wish to ask the good Lord for greater sufferings, for I am too little. They would become my very own sufferings, I would be forced to endure them alone, and I have never been able to do anything all alone."[2]

We hesitate, in any case, to make such a prayer, for we are afraid. To say that we are ready to receive the crosses Jesus will send us, even without asking for the cross, makes us afraid, makes our nature tremble. I understand this well. But it is a magnificent occasion for generosity and confidence. "All you permit for me will be grace from you, and you will be there with me. I do not fear the cross, because I do not fear you, the King of Love." He will never let the cross crush you; on the contrary, it will lift you up toward heaven. It is no longer you who will carry it, it is the cross which will carry you. Jesus took upon himself the bitterest cross and he will add a balm to it before giving it to you—that is certain. The sweetness of the crosses accepted with the joy of free will is a great mystery, yet very real. That is why you must embrace it with open arms. If you hesitate, and drag it along, it will become insupportably heavy. Jesus will withdraw the sweetness from it because you will have turned away from him in turning away from it.

Let us go even further and say that happiness and suffering are inseparable. Some fear to make such an affirmation because the world would look upon them as fools. How can we. say that happiness and suffering are inseparable? Is it not just the other way around? It is not I who say this, but Jesus in the Beatitudes. Open the Gospel to the Sermon on the Mount. What does he tell us? Blessed are those who weep, blessed are the poor, blessed are those who suffer. There then is the affirmation that true happiness and suf-

fering are inseparable. The wisdom we receive straight from
the Divine Master is regarded as foolishness.

The wisdom of the world is exactly opposed to the teach-
ings of the Sermon on the Mount. Jesus says, blessed are
the pure, the world says, blessed are they who indulge in
loose living; Jesus says, blessed are those who weep, the
world says, blessed are those who laugh and amuse themselves; Jesus says, blessed are the meek, the merciful, the
world says, blessed are those who impose themselves on
others and dominate them; Jesus says blessed are the poor,
the world says, blessed are the rich; Jesus says, blessed
are those who suffer, the world says, blessed are those who
enjoy themselves. We must come back to the Sermon on the
Mount. We must not be afraid to say what Jesus said and to
affirm it after him. The Beatitudes are preached too little.
Heaven is spoken of too seldom because Jesus said, blessed
even on this earth, but especially in heaven, didn't he? The
only truly happy people are those who have chosen Jesus
and his cross on earth. They are the thieves of happiness
because they are already happy a hundredfold here below,
and what shall this be for all eternity! To think of heaven
is not egoism, it is to plunge ourselves, with delight, into
the infinite justice and love of God.

In spite of that, remember that Jesus is filled with compassion for those who suffer. He has borne all our sufferings, he has endured them himself at Gethsemane and on
Calvary; but he knows that they are necessary to us, so
"he sends them to us as if with an averted gaze," says
little Thérèse,[3] as if he did not have the courage to watch
us suffer. But he sees at the same time the happiness it
will merit for us, the glory it acquires for his Father, for
him, for us, and the graces it merits for souls; so in love,
in mercy, in tenderness, he hesitates no longer to lay it
upon our poor shoulders, while continuing to sustain it himself, making himself our "Simon of Cyrene."

You see, we are far, very far from the Jansenist notion
of suffering: the chastisement and malediction of a venge-

ful God who crushes us. He is not a vengeful God, but a God full of gentleness who sends us suffering—and with such love! We understand then why he made his beloved Mother the Queen of Martyrs. This is a good example to give those who suffer without comprehending why: "See how he treated his Mother! Did he not love her more than anything in the world? He made her the Queen of Martyrs." Since we shall thank him for all eternity for the time we shall have passed in trial, let us bless him even now.

Must we ask for the cross? No. Must we look for it? No again. Live the doctrine of abandonment which I have preached at such length during this retreat. Accept with thanksgiving everything that happens to you. Say continually," "O Jesus, I thank you for everything." That is enough. Do not ask for crosses, but know how to accept with joy those which Jesus has chosen for you. Besides, crosses will not be lacking. Sanctify yourself with the duties of your state in life, your daily life with all its thorns. Accept all the duties, all the responsibility, with a smile on your lips, a willing smile—a smile that is willed. The most beautiful smiles are those which shine through tears, that we give in spite of ourselves.

Accept the unexpected crosses—they are the most painful: the sickness which immobilizes you, the feeling of being useless and a burden to others, of knowing that while you are needed you are being prevented from doing what you ought to do; the humiliations, contradictions, slanders, calumnies, ingratitude, bad will, criticisms, good intentions misunderstood, family quarrels, very sorrowful bereavements, separations, reverses of fortune. Put up with yourself, with your thousand physical, intellectual, and moral miseries. Accept without complaint the anguish willed by God, as did the Curé of Ars. How many sufferings there are throughout our lives!

Then there is the cross of having carried the cross badly. There is a very practical point here. How many times someone has told me, "I had made a resolution to be generous

in suffering. Then a trial came. I balked, even rebelled.
How many merits I lost!" Thus we add to our original
cross, that of having carried it badly. It is here that we
return to the words of little Thérèse: "We would like to
suffer generously. We would like never to fall—what an
illusion!" See what a lack of logic this is: to moan about
having moaned and then to go on moaning! No! Say to Jesus, "Now I accept the cross you have sent me, which I
at first rejected, and I accept not having accepted it right
away." That is the great resource of humble confidence
pushed to its extreme. You can always, in the present
moment, throw yourself into the arms of Jesus, which are
always open to receive you. It is the present moment which
is so important. In that moment you can take leave of all
the past by giving it to him, in order to bury yourself at
the bottom of his heart.

How many people in the world drag their crosses like a
millstone! A beautiful apostolate to carry out among the
people around you would be to teach them the price of the
cross, and joy in the cross. Souls understand that—they understand all that is divine truth, since they are made, created, and modeled by God to understand it. But we must
learn to show them this with great tact and compassion as
well as conviction.

We must always begin with compassion when we speak to
those who are suffering physically or morally. Begin by
sharing those sufferings. Say, "I understand you. I understand how much you are suffering. I understand your sighs."
Then try by all means to alleviate those sufferings, to care
for the wounds, to be the good Samaritan. If Jesus, who
wept over the tomb of Lazarus, lives in your heart, he himself will inspire you with what to say and do, because that
is what he always has done himself. Compassion, compassion, what a great thing! Mary was associated with Jesus
at Calvary in the Redemption by her loving compassion.
Suffer with those who suffer; do all you possibly can to
help them; comfort them, but always with this same tact,

help them to understand little by little the price of the cross—that there is another life, that if Jesus sends the cross it is always out of love. We will not have enough eternity to thank him for having sent us crosses which will have permitted us to merit in a very small way this beatitude which will be ours and which will never end.

I have heard it put this way: "When Jesus gives me a cross, it is his cross which he really puts on my shoulders, and he is relieved of that much of it."

Another great treasure of suffering is that it teaches us to be compassionate. When one has suffered himself, he understands much better the sufferings of others.

Then too, Jesus distributes sorrows and joys with such great delicacy and tenderness! It has occurred to me to say to him, "It seems to me that you must have a problem with each one of us. You who know the reward of suffering, must will not to withhold it from your elect. On the other hand, you do not have the courage to make them suffer too much. What a dilemma for you! But I know how your heart has resolved it. You draw first of all upon your own unspeakable sufferings and attribute them to us as if they were ours. Then, gently, turning away your head, you share them with us, measuring out our sufferings with sweetness, giving us all the graces we need to bear them. Finally you remind us that love is everything."

There is a certain union of love which is not realized except in shared sorrow. A retreatant confided to me, "On the whole, we go from failure to failure in life. How good it is to know that Jesus, if we are united to him, transforms all these failures into victories!"

Listen to Marie Noël: "What will the Lord give me for our golden wedding anniversary? I quite fear that it will be nothing but a big bouquet of thorns. Those are his own gifts. But I shall receive them and kiss his hands. All the thorns which he has given me have, in the long run, blossomed."[4] There in a few words, a pure poet expresses profound and just truths like a theological thesis, which

go straight to the center of the heart on the wings of poetry.
The Holy Spirit's inspiration can be pure poetry.

St. Peter said, ". . . now you must be for a little time
made sorrowful in divers temptations: that the trial of your
faith (much more precious than gold which is tried by the
fire) may be found unto praise and glory and honor at the
appearing of Jesus Christ" *(1 Pt 1:6)*.

The only real drama is the death of Jesus. All our own
dramas are melted into the great drama of Calvary. But
that is then followed by his Resurrection and ours.

How much good is wrought by this doctrine of love! It
liberates souls so they can make a new start. Their life is
transformed. "All my horizons are changed," they say. "I
see things in a completely different manner than ever before. How much happier I feel!"

Caught up in this net of confidence, the believer rises
from confidence to confidence. A first act of confidence
draws Jesus to him, who enlightens him concerning confidence. Then he plunges himself into it all over again. He
is drawn into a marvelous network, the network of confident love.

Have a very great devotion to that extraordinary sign
which has become too ordinary through routine—the sign
of the cross.

If, each time you make it, you will it and believe it, you
bring upon yourself the infinite goodness of the Father of
Mercies; the Spirit of Love grows in your hearts and you
put on Jesus Christ again *(cf. Rom 13:14)*. You cover yourself instantly with his blood which liberates and purifies
you. You make the Redemption yours. You unite yourself
to the Lamb slain and raised to life, who is always living
to make intercession for you in heaven *(cf. Ap 5:6, Heb 7:25)*.
You glorify the Holy Trinity. One gesture—it takes you a
few seconds, you can make it a hundred times a day—and
it plunges you each time into eternity. There is even a certain physical satisfaction in covering yourself with the sign
of the cross.

Into the divine plan for the death of the Savior on a cross, the thought surely entered of the ease with which we would be able to unite ourselves, by a simple sign made on ourselves, to this mystery of greatest love whereby God gave his life for those he loved *(cf. Jn 15:13)*.

How Jesus has sweetened, embellished, facilitated things for us by so many sufferings! I do not ask you to think of all that each time you make the sign of the cross, but to know it and confidently believe it.

So, learn to make joys of all your crosses. We have only a single, very brief life in which to suffer in loving and to love in suffering: let us not lose a minute of it. John XXIII said on his death bed, "It is good to suffer in loving." If we could regret anything in heaven, it would be to have suffered insufficiently here on earth—the fruitful suffering, the glorious suffering, the cross of Jesus. *Ave bona crux! O crux ave, spes unica!* "Welcome, good cross! Welcome, our one great hope!" Father Damian understood this when he wrote to his superior, "There is no longer any doubt about me. I am a leper. Blessed be God!"

To the question: could Christ have saved us without having suffered and died? St. Thomas[5] answers that his death was, in itself, not at all necessary, but he shows the benefits which the passion procures for us beyond our reconciliation with God.

First of all, by the passion of Jesus Christ man sees how much God loves him and he is thus incited to love God in return; and that is the perfection of the salvation of man.

By his passion Christ gave us an example of humility, of constancy, of justice, of obedience, and of the other virtues necessary for our salvation.

By his passion, he not only liberated man from sin, but he merited for him the grace of justification, glory, and beatitude.

He induces man to keep himself pure and free from sin, according to the words of St. Paul: "For you are bought with a great price. Glorify and bear God in your body" *(1*

Cor 6:20). Man has attained a higher dignity. Misled and
conquered by the devil, man was obliged to conquer him in
turn; having merited death, he had also to triumph over
death by dying. "O death, where is your victory?"

Having himself suffered the trial, Jesus can better help
those who are being tried. Sin is conquered by the love,
"strong as death" *(Ct 8:6)*, of Jesus for his Father and for
us. It was like a conspiracy of merciful love between the
Father and the Son. It is false to think that the Father was
harsh in his treatment of the Son—it is even inconceivable.
No, their common plan was to reunite us to themselves in
the "blood of the covenant."

St. Thomas says again that the death of Christ was not
caused by sin, but by his love, on the occasion of our sins.
It is our sins which crucify Jesus, but they crucify him because he loves us with a merciful love. It is this love which
redeems us and saves us.[6] Jesus delivered himself up out of
love *(cf. Jn 13:1)*. God is love: the death of Jesus is the
great revelation of that fact.

Father F. X. Durrwell makes this luminously clear:[7] The
cross cannot be fully understood except in the perspective
of the Resurrection. . . . The sacrifice of Christ does not
find its fulfillment except in the Resurrection and the glorification of the Savior.

Death and Resurrection share the work of our salvation.
The Resurrection manifested the glory and divinity of the
Savior in his holy humanity. From the glorified body of
Jesus, the Holy Spirit is poured out on the faithful to com-
municate to them the divine life of which the glorification
of Christ is the principle.

This is the heart of the paschal mystery: "For we are
buried together with him by baptism into death: that, as
Christ is risen from the dead by the glory of the Father,
so we also may walk in newness of life" *(Rom 6:4)*.

"Come Holy Spirit, fill the hearts of your faithful and
enkindle in them the fire of your love."

He brings us the divine life by putting fire into our hearts.

This fire is consuming and transforming Love; it is the Holy Trinity burning to save us at whatever cost.

Chapter 9

The Eucharist

〰〰〰〰〰〰〰〰〰〰〰〰〰〰〰〰〰〰〰〰〰〰〰〰〰〰〰〰〰〰

Let us listen first to the words of the Council: "At the Last Supper, on the night when he was betrayed, our Savior instituted the Eucharistic Sacrifice of his body and blood. He did this in order to perpetuate the sacrifice of the Cross throughout the centuries until he should come again, and so to entrust to his beloved spouse, the Church, a memorial of his death and resurrection: a sacrament of love, a sign of unity, a bond of charity, a paschal banquet in which Christ is eaten, the mind is filled with grace, and a pledge of future glory is given to us."[1]

The Mass commemorates the sacrifice of the Cross: "For as often as you shall eat this bread and drink the chalice, you shall show the death of the Lord, until he come" *(1 Cor 11:26)*. But it is not simply a remembrance:"It is truly and properly the offering of a sacrifice, wherein by an unbloody immolation the divine High Priest does what he had already done on the Cross, offering himself to the eternal Father as a most acceptable victim. 'One . . . and the same is the victim, one and the same is he who now offers by the ministry of his priests and who then offered himself on the Cross; the difference is only in the manner of offering.' . . . On the Cross he offered to God the whole of himself and his sufferings, and the victim was immolated by a bloody death voluntarily accepted. But on the altar, by reason of the glorious condition of his humanity, 'death will no longer have dominion over him,' and therefore the shedding of his blood is not possible. Nevertheless the divine wisdom has devised a way in which our Redeemer's sacrifice is marvelously shown forth by external signs symbolic of death. By the 'transubstantiation' of bread into the body of Christ and of wine into his blood both his body and blood are ren-

135

dered really present; but the Eucharistic species under which
he is present symbolize the violent separation of his body
and blood, and so a commemorative showing forth of the
death which took place in reality on Calvary is repeated in
each Mass, because by distinct representations Christ Jesus
is signified and shown forth in the state of victim." [2]

Christ, really present in the holy Mass, offers to the
heavenly Father, under sacramental form, his immolation
on the Cross.

Jesus and all the treasures of heaven are ours on the
altar. I have told you, we must make the merits of Jesus
our own. Where do you find them? On the altar of the Mass
where you receive not only grace, but the Author of grace.
"Every time the memorial of this sacrifice is celebrated,
the work of our Redemption is accomplished." [3]

The Mass is the divine act around which the life of the
Church gravitates and of which she is the radiance; the
center from which she receives all impulses and toward
which she is continually directed; the living source from
which she proceeds and the ocean to which she returns. It
is the sacrifice of the Redemption, at once eternal and per-
petuated in time, in heaven before God and on earth among
us.

Is sacrifice the essential act of all religion by the fact
that the destruction of human life is the absolute homage
due to the supreme majesty and the expression of his dominion over life and death? St. Thomas sees it differently.
He sees God not first of all as the Sovereign Master, but
as the supreme end attracting all beings to himself. He
has nothing to receive from them, but he wills to communicate his goodness to them. *An divitias bonitatis ejus contem-
nis:* "Or do you despise the riches of his goodness?" *(Rom
2:4)*

In a beautiful passage on the Eucharist, Cardinal Charost
writes, "It is to recognize the infinite goodness of God who
is Love, his right to be loved and honored by a supreme
cult, it is to proclaim that God is man's sovereign good, it

is to yield to gratitude—a sentiment still more profound than that of man's dependence—that in the sacrifice man makes a gift of himself, surrenders himself completely to God."

If man had not sinned, the sacrifice would not have been one of blood. Since the fall, man must recognize that death is his due, *stipendia peccati mors*, "the wages of sin are death" *(Rom 6:23)*, and that in offering the victim he wills to reconstitute the order of divine justice. But as injustice is rejection of infinite love, it must be repaired by infinite love.

This infinite love is Jesus who offered it to his Father on the Cross, and continues to offer it in the Eucharist. Unique Priest, unique Victim, immolated by a twofold love: thanksgiving to his Father, and mercy towards us! He wills to satisfy his justice, but above all to content his heart by a superabundant outpouring of love to compensate for the ingratitude of men.

The pages of the Gospel proclaim this eternal love of Jesus for his Father. To make the flame of love mount higher, he feeds it with sorrow. Thus, many souls hide their sacrifice, as Jesus hid his, happy to suffer and die in order to love God better.

You understand then that God does not chastise us as he chastised under the ancient law, although the world of todays seems to be as much as ever under the domination of Satan. That is because there is always, between earth and heaven, a Host which rises like the sun, and which cries, "Father, mercy!" "The Father hears his beloved Son in whom he is well pleased" *(Mt 3:17)* and listens to him.

God created man by love and for his glory; he gave him intelligence that he might know him, a heart that he might love him, and a will that he might serve him. We must contemplate the infinite majesty of God who is, at the same time, our first principle and our last end; it is from him that we receive all that we have and all that we are. We must submit to him our spirit, heart, will, our entire self in adoration, thanksgiving, petition, and, because we are sinners,

expiation. It is the Eucharistic Sacrifice which expresses
these obligations and translates these sentiments. The value
of the Sacrifice is measured by the dignity of the Victim
and the sanctity of the High Priest. There is only one glorious Sacrifice to God: the Incarnate Word.

The holy Mass is therefore perfect adoration, full thanksgiving, satisfaction of infinite value, all-powerful prayer.

Some contemporary theologians have thrown new lights
on the Redemption and the Eucharist which enlighten the
intelligence and warm the heart, for they show us still
more clearly that, as the Curé of Ars preached, "in the
heart of God there is but love."

As Jesus reserved the disclosure of the most intimate
secrets of his Heart in order to warm his people when they
had grown cold through Jansenism, it seems that he reserved these new lights on the Redemption for our era when
atheism is wreaking such great devastation, in order to
draw back to the Holy Church, by the power of love, those
who have been drawn away.

The purposes of the Sacrifice are illumined by the deep-
ened understanding of the blood of the new covenant, shed
for the remission of sins (cf. Mt 26:28, 1 Cor 11:25), and
opening the way to our reconciliation with God. The blood of
the paschal Lamb, the blood of the covenant, expresses the
bond of love which is established between God and his people.

Thus the sacrifice, as well as the paschal meal, is an act
of thanksgiving. Christ fulfills the office of the High Priest,
which is to expiate the sins of the people (Heb. 2:17) by
means of intercession. He is our propitiation (Rom. 3:25,
1 Jn 2:2, 4:10) by which God looks kindly on us, pardons us
our sins, and brings us back to life. Our Redemption was a
liberation through the death and Resurrection of Christ—a
liberation we have received from him, not by payment of
our own ransom to God. As to the fourth purpose of the
Sacrifice, it is the same petition as that of Christ on the
cross who "with a strong cry and tears, offering up prayers
and supplications to him who was able to save him from

death, was heard for his reverence" *(Heb 5:7)*. It is the same as that of the sacrificial lamb, "who is at the right hand of God, who also makes intercession for us" *(cf. Ap 5:6, Rom 8:34, Heb 7:25)*.

St. Paul sees the altar as the source of his confidence: "Having therefore a great high priest who has passed into the heavens, Jesus, the Son of God, let us hold fast our confession, for we have not a high priest who cannot have compassion on our infirmities, but one tempted in all things as we are, without sin. Let us go therefore with confidence to the throne of grace, that we may obtain mercy and find grace in seasonable aid" *(Heb 4:14)*.

Oh! let us not live like abandoned people. If you want to be confident souls, love the Mass ardently. Our Lord has compassion on our miseries, on our weaknesses. He has compassion on all our sufferings. When we are sad at having been unfaithful, he consoles us for having caused him pain. That is how far his merciful tenderness goes. Who will sound the depths of the goodness, the compassion, the condescension of our Savior for us? No, we do not have a high priest who cannot have compassion on our weakness.

"Behold your King who comes to you full of meekness" *(Mt 21:5)*.

Therefore Jesus is our Priest. Priests are not the successors to the priesthood of Jesus Christ, but his ministers. He is the only Host acceptable to the Father.

It is a marvelous thing that Jesus Christ, while still remaining the unique Priest and unique Host, allows these roles to be shared by the consecrated priest and all the faithful. As the Council affirms in *Lumen Gentium,* "Though they differ from one another in essence and not only in degree, the common priesthood of the faithful and the ministerial or hierarchical priesthood are nonetheless interrelated: each of them in its own special way is a participation in the one priesthood of Christ. The ministerial priest, by the sacred power he enjoys, teaches and rules the priestly peo-

ple; acting in the person of Christ, he makes present the
Eucharistic Sacrifice, and offers it to God in the name of all
the people. But the faithful, in virtue of their royal priesthood, join in the offering of the Eucharist. They likewise
exercise that priesthood in receiving the sacraments, in
prayer and thanksgiving, in the witness of a holy life, and
by self-denial and active charity."[4]

But if Christ the Lord made the new people "a kingdom
and priests to God and his Father" *(cf. Ap 1:6, 5:10)*, if
you are "a chosen generation, a kingly priesthood, a holy
nation, a purchased people" *(1 Pt 2:9)*. St. Paul exhorts all
of you, by the mercy of God, "to present your bodies a
living sacrifice, holy, pleasing unto God" *(Rom 12:1)*. See the
grandeur of the simple faithful: priests and victims at the
same time.

I want to speak to you now about the spirit of being a
victim. The word victim frightens us as if it foreboded unhappiness, bitter and despairing suffering. But the victim
of love does not suffer as one suffers who has not given
everything. The two are as different as day and night. The
victim will always be Love's privileged one. If only you
knew the joy with which Jesus fills everything when we
have given him everything! The way he adds pure joys
when there is sorrow, the way he metes out suffering and
happiness with the delicacy of the most tender and compassionate Father, the most loving Friend! If you only knew!
But often he lets it be neither seen nor felt beforehand, in
order that we may receive merit from the very first step.
If, before delivering ourselves up, we were to realize all
the happiness we would find in this total gift of self, we
would not gain the least merit. So Jesus hides it, that we
may merit by confident generosity.

To unite ourselves to the Mass, to offer the Sacrifice,
to consume the Victim, is to say that we would like to be
victims with him. Our Communion at Mass assimilates us to
the Divine Victim. Though mystical members of the immolated Body, most Christians do not realize clearly enough

that they participate in the Redemption in the measure to which they associate themselves with the divine immolation by personal immolation.

In *Mediator Dei* Pius XII said, even before the Council, "But if the oblation whereby the faithful in this Sacrifice offer the divine victim to the heavenly Father is to produce its full effect, they must do something further: they must also offer themselves as victims. . . . In this way every element in the liturgy conspires to make our souls reflect the image of the divine Redeemer through the mystery of the Cross, so that each one of us may verify the words of St. Paul: 'With Christ I hang upon the Cross; and yet I am alive; or rather, not I; it is Christ who lives in me.' We thus identify ourselves with Christ as victim for the greater glory of the Eternal Father. . . . This being so, nothing could be more right and just than that all of us, together with our divine Head who suffered for us, should immolate ourselves to the Eternal Father. . . . 'Through Him, and with Him, and in Him, is given to you, God the Father Almighty, in the unity of the Holy Spirit, all honor and glory for ever and ever.' And as the people answer 'Amen,' let them not forget to offer themselves and their anxieties, their sorrows, their troubles, their miseries and their needs, in union with their divine Head crucified."[5]

What does the Pope mean when he asks all Christians to immolate themselves as victims with the divine Victim of Calvary and of the Mass? How are we to accomplish this desire of the Pope, which is simply the desire of Jesus himself?

We can distinguish two kinds of victims: those who offer themselves to Justice and those who offer themselves to Love. The first desire to satisfy the justice of God by paying for sinners. They are characterized by a call to suffering. Like St. Margaret Mary, they see themselves with all sinners as criminals and deliver themselves to all kinds of anguish in order to appease divine justice. "I do not wish to live any longer," says the saint, "except in order to have

the happiness of suffering. My lot will therefore be to remain on Calvary until the last breath, desiring to be immolated on the altar of the Heart of Jesus, purified, consumed
in the ardor of his flames."

Needless to say, this offering presupposes a tremendous
love. I think that until little Thérèse, the offering as victim was always made, with varying nuances, in this same
spirit.

But Saint Thérèse found another way to offer herself,
another way to immolate herself and die a victim. This
"discovery of love" is something divinely beautiful. She
sees the heart of Jesus overflowing with tenderness and
mercy for poor sinners, for all men; from this heart escape
floods of love which Jesus the Savior cannot contain any
longer. But men in their ingratitude do not want this divine
love. They reject it; they raise the rampart of their indifference, of their contempt, and even of their hatred, so that
the saving flood will not reach them.

What a disappointment this is for Jesus, who is burning
to pour out his love and cannot do it; there is the King,
begging for love, begging for hearts which he can fill with
his merciful tenderness, and finding none—having a heart
overflowing with loving goodness, a longing to share it,
and finding no one who wants to receive it. Love came to
his own and his own did not want to have anything to do
with him. His heart was crushed from the inside, so to
speak, by the love which he could not pour out. So his little
victim presented herself. I want this love which men reject.
I open my heart wide to this divine love; let it invade me,
let it burn me, let it consume my heart completely. Thus I
shall console my divine Savior. Thus I shall die a victim of
love, immolated in this ocean of flames.

"Oh, my God," cries little Thérèse, "will there be nothing
but your justice to receive sacrificial victims from the holocaust? Does not your merciful Love need them also? On
all sides that Love is misunderstood, rejected; the hearts
on which you desire to lavish it turn instead toward crea-

tures, seeking happiness among them instead of throwing themselves into your arms and accepting your infinite love.

"Oh, my God! Will your rejected love remain within your heart? It seems to me that if you found souls offering themselves as sacrificial victims to your love, you would consume them rapidly, you would be happy not to restrain at all the floods of infinite tenderness that are in you. If your justice desires to be satisfied, though it is extended only on earth, how much more does your merciful Love desire to enkindle souls, since your mercy is extended even unto the heavens! Oh, my Jesus, let me be this happy victim, consume your victim in the fire of your divine love!"[6]

Then a marvelous thing happens: when this love which men refuse has passed through the heart of little Thérèse and other victims like her, consuming them, men are no longer able to refuse it! By being a victim of love, she becomes an apostle of Love.

Here again we find the essential truth that the primary apostolate is that of prayer and suffering, of immolation of self by love and in the holocaust in union with Jesus in Gethsemane and on Calvary. Thus sinful man is not forgotten. Little Thérèse was essentially an apostle. "I understood that only love makes the members of the Church act, that if love were ever extinguished, apostles would no longer announce the Gospel, martyrs would refuse to pour out their blood. I understood that Love embraces all vocations, that Love is all"[7]

She recognized in this Love the "twofold love" which contains in its unity the love of God and the love of neighbor. She made her own the words of the Canticle of Canticles, "Draw me: we will run after you to the odor of your ointments." "Just as a torrent, throwing itself impetuously into the ocean, sweeps with it everything that lies in its path, so, O my Jesus, the soul which plunges itself into ᴊhe boundless ocean of your love draws along with itself all that it possesses."[8]

The love of God cannot "consume" the soul unless this

conflagration spreads more and more. Sin is not only ex-
piated, but truly repaired: it is destroyed, effaced in the
soul of the sinner by the infusion of grace, by the fire of
Love.

See what perfect reparation such an offering brings about!
I have mentioned that the great sin of which our Lord complained more than any other to St. Margaret Mary was ingratitude, lack of love. The great reparation therefore is
love—confident love, since the most cruel ingratitude is distrust.

How are we to make this offering real, and live it practically! The most perfect victims are those who let themselves
be immolated by Jesus the High Priest in perfect abandonment, letting him choose the tests, the crosses, the trials,
and also the consolations and joys. It is by all the things he
chooses for them that his love burns and consumes the
hearts which have given themselves to him. Let him be sure
of your smile. To be a victim is to smile. Total abandonment— "O Jesus, I thank you for everything"—that is
enough. Jesus will immolate you in his own way. He will
be the Priest of the host which you will have willed to be
in his hands. I emphasize this point because often I have
been told, "I offered myself, but what must I do now?"
Let him do it! All your life then becomes a Mass in which
you are the host and Jesus the Priest. You have thrown
yourself into the fire, and the fire consumes you continually:
yourself and your miseries.

We must "make a deal" with him, give him *carte blanche*.
In heaven he will recall to us the details of our life of love
with him, forgotten by us, but engraved in his heart; our
small and great pacts with him—especially the great pact
of perfect abandonment.

Sister Geneviève (Céline) writes, "The soul which offers
itself to love does not ask for suffering, but, in delivering
itself up entirely to the designs of love, it accepts all that
Providence permits for it of joys, labor, trials, and it counts
on infinite mercy for everything."

Finally one last thought: what should you do in your incapacity, your powerlessness to make reparation, from which you suffer like all the saints? Offer him his own heart, his own love, the only means by which you can realize your immense desire to love him.

When St. Margaret Mary found herself at a loss as to what more to do to give him reparation which would be worthy of him, to thank him, she offered him his own heart, his own love.

It is always great wisdom to substitute Jesus for ourselves. He desires only that. He came to earth for that.

We can offer something infinite to an infinite Love: the very heart of infinite Love. Make reparation with the Heart of Jesus—he is yours—and always with and through Mary, who makes perfect reparation through her pierced Immaculate Heart. Jesus gave us his heart and the heart of his Mother: they are our divine treasure. "Jesus, I have much to give you, I have everything to give you, I have something infinite to give you: your own love, your heart and the heart of your Mother which is also mine."

Communion

The Eucharistic Sacrifice is therefore "the sacrament of love, the sign of unity, the bond of charity," and at the same time "the paschal banquet in which Christ is consumed, his passion is recalled, the soul is filled with graces and the promise of future glory is given."

Let us come back to the words of Jesus himself, for no words move our hearts like his:

"I am the living bread which came down from heaven. If any man eat of this bread, he shall live for ever: and the bread that I will give is my flesh, for the life of the world. The Jews therefore strove among themselves, saying, How can this man give us his flesh to eat? Then Jesus said to them: Amen, amen, I say unto you, except you eat the flesh of the Son of man and drink his blood, you shall not have life in you. He who eats my flesh and drinks my blood has everlasting life: and I will raise him up in the last day. For my flesh is meat indeed: and. my blood is drink indeed. He who eats my flesh and drinks my blood abides in me: and I in him. As the living Father has sent me and I live by the Father: so he who eats me, the same also shall live by me. This is the bread that came down from heaven. Not as your fathers did eat manna and are dead. He who eats this bread shall live for ever" *(Jn 6:51-59)*.

"You fed your people with the food of angels," says Wisdom, "and gave them bread from heaven, prepared without labor; having in it all that is delicious and the sweetness of every taste" *(Wis 16:20)*.

Paul VI in his admirable encyclical, *Mysterium Fidei*, after having contemplated seven modes of Jesus' presence in his Church, writes: "The mind is filled with amazement at these different ways in which Christ is present; they confront the Church with a mystery ever to be pondered. But there is yet another manner in which Christ is present in his Church, a manner which surpasses all the others; it is his presence in the Sacrament of the Eucharist, . . . it contains Christ himself." And further, "Not only while the sacrifice is offered and the sacrament is received, but as long as the Eucharist is kept in our churches, Christ is truly the Emmanuel, that is, 'God with us,' Day and night he is in our midst, he dwells with us, full of grace and truth."

The apostle St. John, when he speaks of the Last Supper, searches for a word in which he can express all the love which Jesus unveiled at his last supper with the disciples, and he says, *in finem dilexit,* "he loved them unto the end" *(Jn 13:1)*. He loves us to the extreme limits of Love.

Why did Jesus remain with us in the Eucharist? To be our food: he knew how our feeble souls would need this bread of heaven which is himself. He remained in order not to leave us alone. When a person loves, he desires the presence of the beloved.

Leaving aside pure theology, let us imagine that, as he considered the fact that he would have to return to heaven after his Resurrection, there was a conflict in his heart. He did will to die, but he did not want to leave. He did not want to go away from us and leave us alone.

Besides remaining in us by grace, by faith, hope, and charity, he wanted to give us the sweetness and richness of his ineffable presence in the Eucharist, and to remain there with us until the end of time. He would go back, of course, to the glorious heaven to which his glorified body was to return, but at the same time, he would remain. So there was the Cenacle. At the banquet of love in the Cenacle, surrounded by his friends, his brothers, he worked the miracle much greater than creation: he instituted the Holy Eucharist.

He remained in order to be our food: "For my flesh is meat indeed and my blood is drink indeed" *(Jn 6:55)*, a food extraordinary in its effects. He comes into us in order to transform us into himself. He willed more than a union, more than a fusion; he willed the unity of love: to be one with us. The Fathers of the Church search for comparisons to explain this union: two pieces of wax which, when mixed, are no longer distinguishable one from the other; the iron reddened in the fire, which becomes fire itself. Yet it is even more than that. In these there is only union, only fusion, but he truly brings about the oneness of love.

The Council tells us, "The partaking of the body and blood of Christ does nothing other than to cause us to be transformed into that which we consume."[9]

"He assumed our nature in order to communicate to us his divinity; he took a human life in order to give us a part in his divine life; he made himself man in order to make us gods. And his human birth became the means of our birth into the divine life."[10]

See how beautiful it is and how far it goes: he gives us the commandment: "Be you therefore perfect as your heav-

enly Father is perfect" *(Mt 5:48)*. But how? By eating and
drinking the body and blood of him who alone is perfect as
the Father and who transforms us into himself.

In the presence of this Sacrifice and around this holy
table the unity of the people of God is realized, whose "spiritual center" is the Tabernacle, because it contains him
who is the center of all hearts, "by whom are all things,
and we by him" *(1 Cor 8:6)*.

Seek to be Eucharistic souls! Hunger and thirst to eat
this living miracle; nourish yourselves with it! Never omit
receiving Communion through lack of love, through scruples
or fear. From the moment when you are in the state of
grace, go to the holy table, go to receive Jesus! An act
of humility and an act of love prepare you in an instant.
If you cannot go for a reason beyond your control, it is all
right; Jesus will supply, seeing your ardent desire to receive him.

Here is a good thought which is not often mentioned:
receive Communion not only for yourself, in order to have
this immense grace, but for him, in order to respond to
his desire to come down into you, to give him the joy of
descending into your heart, which is a heaven for him.
Perhaps you will say, "What? My poor heart, so miserable,
so unworthy, a heaven for Jesus?" Yes, if you call upon
him to make your heart a heaven for himself.

Here we must remember that sensible love is nothing
in itself. It could be that before and after Communion you
will be cold and distracted. But listen to little Thérèse: "I
cannot say that I have often received consolations during
my thanksgivings; that is perhaps the moment when I have
had the fewest. I find that completely natural since I have
offered myself to Jesus, not as a person who desires to receive his visit for my own consolation, but on the contrary,
for the pleasure of him who gives himself to me. It is not
in order to remain in the golden ciborium that he comes
down each day from heaven, but in order to find another
heaven, the heaven of our souls, made in his image, the

living temple of the adorable Trinity.''[11]

A Lamb—a being even more gentle than a lamb—invites you to receive him and takes away all your sins. Lord, I am not worthy to receive you, but speak only a word, a single word, and I shall be purified—my soul, my heart—by this word which you have spoken, and I will become truly a heaven for you.

These words, ''Behold the Lamb of God who takes away sins,'' and ''I am not worthy, but speak only a word,'' are the most beautiful, the most complete, and the most marvelous preparation for Communion.

Here we see the incomparable richness and depth of the liturgical prayers. They say everything, as long as we recognize their full sense with faith and love.

If you only knew how Jesus hungers for you, how he burns with desire to come into your heart, how impatient he is to come down to you, bridging all distance between you and him! The day you miss a Communion is a great disappointment for him. So go to him, respond to his desire. *Desiderio desideravi.* ''I have desired with a great desire to eat this Pasch with you. I thirst, I thirst for you to come to me; I thirst to come down into you.'' Never deprive him of this happiness through your own fault.

The most beautiful morning prayer, on days when you have not been able to receive Communion because of work or health, is a spiritual communion. Renew in the course of your day this act of real and intimate union with him who is the bread of life: our daily bread in holy Communion. Live in a state of spiritual communion.

Say like St. Margaret Mary, ''Jesus, you know that I am ready to walk barefoot on a path of flames in order not to miss a single Communion.'' Let this be the disposition of your heart even if you do not feel the ardor, the fervor, the desire. Let this be your disposition of soul: to be willing to do anything in order not to miss a single Communion.

It is this disposition that Jesus sees in you, which delights him and attracts him into the heaven of your heart.

On the day when St. Margaret Mary, not being able to receive Communion because she was sick, told him of her immense desire to receive him, in the words I have just quoted, Jesus said to her, "For you alone I would have instituted the Sacrament of my love."

At the moment of receiving Communion, say to Jesus, "Jesus, I come to you because I am weak, because I am miserable, because I am a sinner. I come to you because I have so much need of you." What a beautiful preparation for Communion! Do not say to him, "I come to you because I am well prepared," but, "I come to you because I need you so much."

It is an exclusive right of the weak and miserable to be able to pray this prayer, with even greater fervor: "I need you and I am happy to be in such great need of your mercy:" a prayer which goes like an arrow straight to the depths of his infinitely merciful heart.

Let your Mass be the center of your day. Everything must flow for you from your daily Mass and everything must culminate in it. Your day, because you will have willed it, must be a thanksgiving for the Mass you attended in the morning and a preparation for the Mass you will attend the next day.

That does not mean you should think all day about your morning Mass or that of the next day; it means that you will have said to Jesus, making these words your disposition of soul: "I want all my life to be centered on the altar of the Mass, to depend on it, and to culminate in it, to be a thanksgiving and a preparation for my daily Mass. All my life, all my days, all the beatings of my heart."

As apostles, never forget that your spiritual and supernatural fruitfulness will come always and above all else from the Mass, and then from your personal immolation united to that of the altar.

Be apostles of holy Mass and Communion. Do everything possible to facilitate daily Communion. Invite children to communicate as often as possible. Think of Jesus' desire to descend into souls, of the happiness he finds there, of the eternal consequences for a single soul, to have received one more holy Communion during its passage on earth. Have an ardent desire for Jesus in the Host.

St. Pius X, the latest canonized pope, was the promoter of daily Communion. In his saintly heart he realized what Mass and Communion are. Urge souls to come! Do everythink in your power to see that the souls confided to your care have a Eucharistic life as complete and as total as possible. Reserve as many moments as you can to visit and adore the Blessed Sacrament.

Adoro te devote. "Devoutly I adore you."[12]

Jesus became "someone" for all the villagers at Ars tnrough the preaching and example of St. John Vianney. "He is there, he is there," repeated the Curé of Ars, pointing to the tabernacle. The girls no longer dared to hold their revels on the knoll behind the sanctuary, for they knew that Jesus was there. They perceived the Real Presence as if sensibly, and they too said, "He is there."

Well known is the account of the peasant of Ars who, when his Curé noticed him spending hours in the church and asked him what he said to God, replied, "I do not say anything. I look at him and he looks at me." It will remain one of those responses that only the simple and the little ones know how to give, and which say much more than many theses.

Be souls of prayer who seek to imitate Jesus. "And he retired into the desert and prayed" *(Lk 5:16)*. "He went out to a mountain to pray: and he passed the whole night in the prayer of God" *(Lk 6:12)*. "And going a little further, he fell upon his face, praying" *(Mt 26:39)*.

Saints, masters in spirituality, have spoken admirably about prayer, especially since St. John of the Cross and St. Teresa of Avila, to tell of its capital importance, its fruitfulness, its necessity.

In concluding this already lengthy conference, let me return once again to little Thérèse and speak briefly of her.

Alluding to Archimedes, who said, "Give me a lever and a fulcrum and I shall lift the world," she thought that what Archimedes was not able to achieve, the saints had accomplished: "The Omnipotent gave them their leverage point— himself alone—and prayer for a lever, the prayer which inflames with the fire of love; and with these, they lifted the world."[13]

"How great is the power of prayer," she cried. "like a queen who has free access at all times to the king, and can obtain all she asks."

Leaving aside the prefabricated prayers which made her head ache, she said, "I do it like the children who do not know how to read. I simply say to God what I want to say to him, without making beautiful sentences, and he always understands me. Prayer is a movement of the heart, a simple look cast toward heaven, a cry of recognition and love in the midst of trial as in the midst of joy; finally, it is something great and supernatural which expands my soul and unites me to Jesus."[14]

"All that does not prevent distractions and sleep from coming to visit me, but I always know how to find the means to be happy and profit from my miseries."[15]

In her weakness, Holy Scripture and the *Imitation of Christ* helped her. She found in them solid and completely pure nourishment, but it was the Gospels above all which bore her up during these prayers. There she always discovered new insights, hidden and mysterious meanings.[16]

Yet sensing Jesus in her, guiding her every moment, inspiring in her what she must say or do, she discovered—as the fruit of her union with Jesus in complete abandonment— the lights which she had not yet received, just at the moment she needed them, and she adds, "it is not usually during my prayers that they are most abundant, but rather in the midst of the occupations of the day."[17]

How balanced and profound this is! With what authority, assurance and wisdom little Thérèse sweeps away the illusions in the spiritual life! She knew very well that, "No one can say Jesus is Lord except by the action of the Holy Spirit" *(1 Cor 12:3)*.

"Likewise, the Spirit also helps our infirmity. For we know not what we should pray for as we ought: but the Spirit himself asks for us with unspeakable groanings" *(Rom 8:26)*.

It is the Holy Spirit who contemplates and prays in us. To make a prayer, to pray, is to think lovingly of God. The Holy Spirit is Love.

How did men receive the Eucharist, this gift of incomprehensible love? On Holy Thursday Jesus went directly from the Cenacle to the Mount of Olives. There, as he sweated blood, his greatest suffering—as he confided to St. Margaret Mary—was the ingratitude of men, especially their ingratitude toward the Sacrament of his love.

He saw in advance the long days, the long nights when he would be alone, forgotten, in thousands of tabernacles in solitary churches, the thousands of indifferent people who would pass each day before the churches without even thinking for an instant that he is there, those who would enter the churches to admire the windows, the architecture, yet not make even a little genuflection before the tabernacle. He saw the multitude of the baptized, whom he was to make his adopted children in his blood, who would neglect even Sunday Mass, who would fail to receive Easter Communion. After delivering himself up in the Host, as he did, what does he ask of us? A half hour a week, on Sunday; one Communion each year. Could he have required less? He gives without counting the cost, asking a tiny return, and he is refused.

He saw in advance the sacrilegious Communions, the hatred with which he was to be pursued, especially in the Eucharist, by the impious members of diabolical sects. He saw all that in advance. He foresaw everything in Gethsemane, and he accepted it all, that he might descend into a single soul who loves him. "For you alone I would have instituted the Sacrament of my love."

The model of the abandonment I have preached to you

at such length is the Host. The priest puts it on the left,
it remains on the left. He places it on the right, it remains
on the right! Those who profane it come, they take him
from his tabernacle and throw him into the gutter; he lets
himself be thrown into the gutter. This is our lesson in perfect abandonment. He is not only the model, but also the
source of it.

You will not live this life of holiness, confidence, abandonment, and peace which I have preached to you so far, except in the measure to which you drink at the fountain of
living water, the fountain which flows unto eternal life, the
fountain of the altar.

The Enthronement

In the spirit of its founder, there is such an intimate con-
nection between the "Enthronement of the Sacred Heart of
Jesus in the home" and the Eucharist, that I would like to
say a few words here about this wholly supernatural work
which falls well within the scope of this retreat.

The Enthronement was founded by Father Mateo Craw-
ley, at the beginning of the century.

Born in Peru, in 1875, of an English father and a Peru-
vian mother, he studied at Valparaiso, in Chile, in a college
directed by the French Fathers of the Congregation of the
Sacred Hearts of Jesus and Mary and of the Perpetual
Adoration of the Most Holy Sacrament of the Altar. This
congregation, which has two branches, fathers and sisters,
was founded at Poitiers, right in the midst of the revolu-
tion, by Father Coudrin and Mother Henriette Aymer de
la Chevalerie.

Since they had received from heaven inestimable graces
of the Heart of Jesus and the Heart of Mary—inseparable
from one another and from the Eucharist—it is a congregation obviously dedicated to Love.[18] Having entered this congregation upon completion of his studies, Father Mateo received through it the graces which were to make him the

world-wide apostle of the Heart of Jesus.

He was in fact an·extraordinary apostle. For nearly a half century, he travelled continuously throughout western Europe, the Far East, and the two Americas, preaching in six languages, visiting twenty-two nations, contacting more than one hundred thousand priests, bringing together a million faithful in the nocturnal adoration in the home, enthroning the Sacred Heart in millions of families.

He certainly received a mission and the graces to fulfill it. He possessed a very special natural personal radiance— for he was very gifted—but especially a supernatural radiance. He had much of the penetrating tenderness of St. John, the ardent and conquering faith of St. Paul, and the burning love for Jesus which both possessed. He had the gift of attracting crowds and when a person had met him and heard him once, he never forgot him.[19]

The Enthronement is the response to the words of Jesus in the Apocalypse: "Behold, I stand at the gate and knock. If any man shall hear my voice and open to me the door, I will come in to him and will sup with him: and he with me" *(Ap 3:20).*

It is Jesus received by Zaccheus: "This day is salvation come to this house. . . . For the Son of Man is come to seek and to save that which was lost" *(Lk 19:9).* It is Bethany.

The whole family, in its plurality and its unity, lives this divine intimacy—of which I have spoken so often in these last days—with Jesus the adored King and incomparable Friend. The Council tells us: ". . . the Creator of all things has established conjugal society as the beginning and basis of human society. . . . This mission—to be the first and vital cell of society—the family has received from God. It will fulfill this mission if it appears as the domestic sanctuary of the Church by reason of the mutual affection of its members and the prayer that they offer to God in common, if the whole family makes itself a part of the liturgical worship of the Church, and if it provides active hospitality and promotes justice and other good works for the service of all the brethren in need."[20] That is the central idea of the Enthronement: "the family, this little church, of which the father is the bishop," as St. Augustine so aptly put it.

"Thus the Christian family, which springs from marriage as a reflection of the loving covenant uniting Christ with the Church, and as a participation in that covenant, will manifest to all men Christ's living presence in the world, and the genuine nature of the Church. This the family will do by the mutual love of the spouses, by their generous fruitfulness, their solidarity and faithfulness, and by the loving way in which all members of the family assist one another."[21]

The Council tells us again that "Since Christ, sent by the Father, is the source and origin of the whole apostolate of the Church, the success of the lay apostolate depends upon the laity's living union with Christ . . . that while correctly fulfilling their secular duties in the ordinary conditions of life, they do not separate union with Christ from their life but rather, performing their work according to God's will, they grow in that union."[22] For the family will live from an apostolic and missionary spirit. It will be the cradle *par excellence* of vocations.

But Father Mateo saw further than the sanctification of the family. The great goal which he pursued was the actualization of the reign of the Sacred Heart in society, bringing all of society to his love, family by family.

Here is what he says: "The Enthronement of the Sacred Heart in the home is the homage of adoration, of social reparation, and of fervent love, which the family as a cell of society renders to the Heart of Jesus, as the King of society. It never ceases to reconquer all of society for Jesus Christ by enthroning him at the sources of life, at the basis of society, the home. When Jesus Christ is not the king, the center of hearts in our family and social life, nothing can long resist the storm of passions. Authentic and lasting peace does not come, cannot come except by him, the Prince of Peace. Jesus is the sole reality. Sooner or later all creatures fail us. . . . He alone never deceives; he alone is faithful; he alone is the strength, the support, the unique Friend. Redouble your Eucharistic fervor! We must form profoundly Eucharistic families by the Enthronement in order to form strongly Christian societies, Christian not only on the surface and by custom, but in spirit and in truth.

"Nocturnal adoration in the home constitutes the sinews of our holy war. Keep to it with all the ardor of your heart. Enthronement is living and lived primarily by this ardor.

"Love the Heart of Jesus, love him foolishly, love him above all things, immersing all your affections in him without fear of sacrifice. The Heart of Jesus is an abyss which does not divide. We love more, we love better when we love Jesus. Natural affection is transformed, made greater made God-like.

"Love is the entire gospel: it is the entire Jesus, in the arms of his mother and the arms of the Cross." [23]

Chapter 10

Jesus, Mary, the Saints

Throughout this retreat I have asked the Immaculate Queen to comment on it herself in the intimacy of your souls, to bring Jesus closer to you, or rather to open your eyes to his adorable presence, for he is always with you. My whole intention has been to give him to you in a more profound way and to plunge your hearts for time and eternity into his Heart, the abyss of fire and blood opened for you.

But that is the work of Mary. Jesus has belonged to Mary since her *Fiat* ("Be it done.") in Nazareth. It is her prerogative to give him to you and it is also through her that he wills to receive your gifts and especially your hearts. May she hide you in his Heart and keep you there forever.

I would like to present to you in a few words five of the most beautiful jewels in the Heart of Mary: her simplicity, her abandonment, her love for the Cross, her thirst for souls, her love.

The Gospel tells us nothing about the childhood of Mary. It seems that God willed jealously to hide this diamond of greatest beauty. And Mary, all her life, kept her love of reticence, of self-effacement, of the hidden life, under the veil of simplicity, like a marvelous treasure. Think of her at Nazareth, the wife of a carpenter, keeping the household, sweeping, going to the fountain, she, the Queen of Heaven. She appears later as if lost in the midst of the holy women, having nothing to distinguish her. I do not see Mary fainting in the arms of St. John or Mary Magdalene, but standing —*Stabat Mater* ("His Mother stood")—in immense sorrow and in divine peace. After laying Jesus in the tomb, St. John brought Mary back to his own home *(cf. Jn 19:27)* where she was to live, until the Assumption, the same life she had led at Nazareth.

I picture to myself Mary during the discourse of St. Peter on the morning of Pentecost; no one in the crowd of hearers had any idea that the mother of this resurrected Jesus, of whom St. Peter told them, the Mother of God, the Spouse of the Holy Spirit who inflamed their hearts, was there, silent, in their midst.

Mary is the most imitable of all the saints. If I search the catalogue of the saints for a model of the most humble and poorest of women on earth, I find not a single one who is more truly this model than Mary.

Little Thérèse rediscovered this road of Nazareth. She approached this simplicity, but without equalling it—far from it. At Carmel there is still the austerity of the religious habit, of the enclosure. At Nazareth there was none of that.

In our time Jesus also wants hidden saints like the "woman of Nazareth," who distinguish themselves in nothing exteriorly, but who burn interiorly. Never, moreover, have there been more saints of this kind than in our day.

Mary's second jewel is her total abandonment: her living and limitless faith. The angel brings her the phenomenal announcement: she will be the mother of the Messiah; the Son of God will be her Son. Seeing her moved in her humility, and not understanding how she will remain a virgin, the angel reassures her, "The Holy Spirit will come upon you and the power of the Most High will overshadow you" *(Lk 1:35)*. He reminds her that nothing is impossible to God. He gives her a sign. God has spoken and the response pours forth from the depths of the soul of Mary: "Behold the handmaid of the Lord, be it done to me according to your word." This is the *Fiat* of Mary, pronounced in the name of all humanity. Without her we would not have Jesus, we would not have our Brother, our Friend, our Savior. The loving abandonment of Mary is at the origin of our Redemption.

At the origin of the redemption of those souls whom God has resolved to save through you must be also your loving abandonment, your *Ecce ancilla*, ("Behold the handmaid,") your *Fiat*. He asks us to pronounce these words very often each day, which sometimes cost our feeble nature so much, with unreserved acceptance of the divine will, whatever it be—so often crucifying yet always to be held in adoration.

The third jewel is her heroism of the Cross.

Jesus told St. Margaret Mary, "From the first moment of my Incarnation, the Cross was planted in my heart." We might well think that at the same moment it was also planted in the Heart of Mary. She knew the Scriptures too well not to know that her Son would be "the Man of Sorrows" of Isaias, that she would see him one day with "no beauty in him, nor comeliness, . . . despised and the most abject of men, . . . wounded for our iniquities: bruised for our sins" *(Is 53:3, 5)*. She very soon received confirmation from Simeon's announcement: "Your own soul a sword shall pierce" *(Lk 2:35)*. What must she not have felt at the time of the massacre of the Innocent One whom she carried in her arms and pressed to her heart.

The abnegation of Mary appeared again in two separations from Jesus. It is so hard to leave those we love! She had already known a sorrowful separation at the moment of the death of St. Joseph. The Gospel does not speak of it, but we can picture to ourselves the first departure of Jesus from Nazareth. She had the certainty of his coming death. Finished were the long conversations with her Son, the unspeakable sweetness of the exchanges between two hearts so marvelously exquisite, sensitive, delicate, radiant with tenderness, as were the Heart of Jesus and the Heart of Mary. All that was ended for this earthly life.

Then there was the separation of Calvary, when she witnessed with her eyes, with her broken heart, the full reality. She saw the soldiers strip him of his clothes, tear to shreds the adorable flesh she had given him, pound nails into the hands she had so often held in her own and kissed with adoration. What an exchange it was when Jesus gave her to St. John! "She received," says St. Bernard, "the servant for the Lord, the disciple for the Master, the son of Zebedee in exchange for the Son of God!" He adds, "The thrust of the sword did not reach the soul of Jesus, for he was dead, but it reached the very depths of the soul of Mary." But Mary said, without hesitation, in her spirit, in her will, in her heart, *Fiat, Magnificat*. She knew that all these crosses were, in the divine plan, necessary for the salvation of men and the greatest proof of love which Jesus could give her. By these separations, Mary was preparing for the great reunion of the Assumption, when she was to see the wounds streaming with blood changed into wounds streaming with light and glory.

The fourth jewel is her thirst for souls. Mary is the Queen of the Apostles. She is an apostle in a different way, because each soul to be saved is a child of hers. In her *Fiat* at Nazareth there is something of the impulse of a mother who wants to prevent her child from falling into the flames, for she realized more than anyone else what sin is, what hell is. So she cried, "Yes, let me receive the sword, the piercing lance at Golgotha. I consent to see Jesus suffer and die to save my other children."

St. Thomas of Villanova says that two loves existed in her: the love of Jesus and the love of men. Her heart as the mother of men prevailed. She loved men so much that she delivered up her only Son for them. In a certain manner, the words of Scripture apply also to her: "For God so loved the world as to give his only begotten Son" *(Jn 3:16)*. But the two loves in the heart of Mary were not in conflict, for it was from her love for Jesus that she drew this love for men which was stronger than death. In Mary, as in Jesus, everything converged toward a single goal: the salvation of poor sinners. Thus Mary is Mediatrix by her cooperation in the unique mediation of the Redeemer.[1]

The fifth jewel of the Heart of Mary is her pure love. This is the diamond which flashes its splendor on all the others. It is more than a jewel of her Heart—it is her Heart itself. The love of Mary explains everything: the *Fiat* of Nazareth which made her the Mother of God, the *Fiat* of Calvary which made her our Mother. Mary was all love because she was completely pure. Purity is not only exemption from any stain, from any sin. Purity is too often made synonymous with the absence of sin. What an error it is to stop there! To drive away darkness we need light. The absence of sin is a condition; but what we need beyond that is the positive beauty of sanctifying grace—that is to say, the Holy Trinity in us. That is purity: Mary, full of grace.

Always go to Jesus through Mary, but not for fear of Jesus. Often in books of piety, Jesus is presented as a judge and Mary as the merciful mother. Yet it is not like that at all because if Mary has a merciful heart, a heart of ineffable tenderness, it is Jesus who gave it to her. He has, even more than she, the heart of a mother. No, this is not the reason why we must always go to Jesus through Mary, but because it is his plan of love. In the same way that he himself came through Mary, he wants us to go to him through Mary. It is the surest way, the most direct way, the sweetest way, too. Why? Because we find Jesus in the arms of Mary.

Then too, he looks much more at the giver than the gift. Let it be Mary who presents him all our gifts, and above all the gift of ourselves. It is because they spring from the mercy of God that the maternal gentleness and tenderness of Mary, my Mother, my Sister, my Queen, are for me so sweet and so tender—not because I see them as contrasting with divine justice. The Holy Spirit in us often works by attraction. What attraction I feel toward Mary—the attraction of a child for his mother! Happily, fervently, lovingly I hide myself under her mantle, I nestle in her arms, on her heart, blending my love with the love of the Father, her Father, for her, with the love of Jesus, her Son, for her, with the love of the Holy Spirit, her Spouse, for her. Everything is tenderness, gentleness, mercy; everything is shared, everything is love. No, it is not in fear of God that I go to Mary, but in love for him, and at the same time in love for her, in order to share everything with them.

Each morning at Mass, the focal point of your days and

of your life, put Jesus on the altar of the wounded Heart of Mary, the Mother of the Church. Assist at Mass near her, with her, at the foot of the Cross, like St. John and St. Mary Magdalene. Love to recite the rosary, meditating on the mysteries. Little Thérèse, said that each Hail Mary goes up toward heaven like incense whose smoking spirals are all alike, though it is always new incense which burns. Love always says the same things, yet never repeats itself. I have already told you, in speaking about Communion, that your heart is a heaven for Jesus, and this is even more so when Jesus finds Mary there. It is her Heart which will reveal to you the intimate secrets of the Heart of Jesus, as it is the Heart of Jesus which will reveal to you the Heart of Mary. Do for the Gospel of Mary what Mary did for the Gospel of Jesus—ponder these things in your heart, or rather, let it be Mary who keeps these things in your heart, all you have heard during the retreat, and reap from them the fruits of eternity.

Yes, it is Mary who will teach you to know Jesus. He is not loved because he is not known. How many there are who do not know Jesus, even among those who call themselves his friends! In the measure in which we place distance between ourselves and him, our blindness increases, the darkness grows about us, it is night and death. He is the light of the world! What can we see, what can we understand without him? The nearer we draw to him, and the more we look at him with the eyes of faith and especially with the eyes of love, the more we say to him, "You are my all, you are my way, you are my truth, you are my life, the life of my life, the soul of my soul." And the more he grows in you, and the more he enlightens you, the more he transforms you and fills you with divine life. This is what the saints have done, and always will do. Why were they heroic? Because, looking at Jesus, knowing him, seeing him in all his beauty, nothing seemed to them too painful, too hard, or too difficult in order to possess him. They were irresistibly attracted to him.

We must be borne up by love. It is impossible to be generous if we are not borne up by love. It is Jesus who must do things in me. He does them, in the measure to which I am intimately united to him. We must charge him with everything, put our burdens upon him. I have told you often during this retreat how necessary it is that Jesus be substituted for us. It is he who must do what we cannot do. We return here to the great cry of the gospel about which I spoke to you the first day: "Come to me, all you who labor and are burdened: and I will refresh you" *(Mt 11:28).*

I am incapable of being faithful or generous if he does not do these things in me, if I am not carried by him.

When I took my religious vows, I said to Jesus, "I am making my vows, but this is above all an act of confidence, because it is you who must keep them. I can never have the courage to bind myself—to make vows for the rest of my life. It is you who must keep them in me. It is you who will do everything."

Sanctity is Jesus growing in us while we die to creatures and to ourselves, Jesus taking all the room in us until we are transformed into him. What a divine lesson we can learn on this subject from the saints! In what union they lived with him on earth! They began here by grace what they continue in eternity in glory: to contemplate and to love their Lord and their God.

Take St. Peter for example. From their first encounters, Jesus takes possession of him: "You are Simon the son of Jona. You shall be called Cephas, which is interpreted Peter" *(Jn 1:42).*

Some days afterwards, Jesus climbs into the boat with Peter to teach the people. Then, having stopped speaking, he said: *Duc in altum*— "Launch out into the deep" *(Lk 5:4).* "Let us embark together, on the ocean of love. You, Peter, go with me out into the depths and then, because to love me is to love as I do, and to love souls with me, throw out your net." Peter had caught nothing all night. With Jesus in his boat, he took in a great quantity of fish

in a moment *(cf. Lk 5:6).* What folly it is to fish without
Jesus! When we fish with him we can be sure of taking in
a prodigious number of souls.

Jesus continued to grow in the heart of Peter. "I shall
give my life for you," said St. Peter. "Lord, to whom shall
we go? Thou hast the words of eternal life" *(Jn 6:68).*
Yet even so Peter denied him because he counted too much
on himself. He had great natural qualities: authority, initiative, decision, zeal. His great mistake, his great error, was
to depend on his own gifts. He needed a lesson. So he got
one—but love saved him: in the look of Jesus when he was
at the court of Caiaphas *(cf. Lk 22:61)* he read not reproach,
but mercy. He was saved.

I have often meditated upon these two looks of Jesus in
the gospel: his look at the rich young man who approached
him and asked,"Good Master, what shall I do to gain eternal
life?" When Jesus enumerated the commandments to him,
he replied, "Master, all these things I have observed from
my youth." The gospel reports that Jesus looked with love
upon this young man who had been so faithful, so generous
(cf. Mk 10:21). He said to him, "One thing is wanting to
you. Go, sell whatever you have and give to the poor: and
you will have treasure in heaven. And come, follow me."
The young man was very rich, and had not the courage to
sacrifice all his possessions. What confusion he must have
experienced when he arrived in heaven and saw who it
was that he had left for such ephemeral riches!

Then I think of the second look of Jesus, after the denial
of Peter. Peter had denied him three times, blaspheming.
In spite of everything! Even after all he had seen, after all
the proofs of love which his Divine Master had given him!
The sin of Peter is truly a frightful sin: to deny with im-
precations him who loved him so much, whom he loved from
the depths of his heart. What cowardice!

The cock crowed, and Jesus turned toward Peter. He gave
him a look of reproach, yes, but of a reproach full of mercy,
a reproach so tender that the soul of Peter was pierced to

the depths. He received grace, he received mercy, he repented, he wept, and was more filled with grace afterwards
then if he had not denied Christ.

See how Jesus builds his great works, his masterpieces
of love, on our misery! St. Peter, chosen to be the first
pope, the pillar of his Church, he permitted to fall so low in
order to make him greater still through mercy.

The glance of love bestowed on the beautiful soul of the
young man in the gospel did not bring the victory of love,
yet the glance upon the sinful soul of St. Peter did bring
the victory. So I ask, "Jesus, bestow on me, poor, miserable
sinner that I am, that glance of mercy which brings victory."

But you will not be intimate with Jesus unless you know
him well and know him as he is. The story of John the
beloved resting upon his Heart must be your story. Why was
St. John so audacious with Jesus? Because it was he who
knew Jesus best. On the breast of the Master he learned to
know him still better. The better he knew him, the more he
leaned upon his Heart; and the more he leaned upon his
Heart, the better he knew him. He certainly knew him better
than the others. Recall the scene of the miraculous draft of
fish. The apostles had fished all night and caught nothing. In
the morning someone appeared on the shore who cried to
them, "Throw the net to the right." They threw the net to
the right side and instantly took up a great quantity of
fish. Immediately St. John recognized him: *Dominus est*—"It
is the Lord" *(Jn 21:7)*. These are the intuitions of the heart.
"*It is the Lord!*" St. Peter had not recognized him, but St.
John had. In the current of your daily life, in the course of
your days, you also must say, "It is the Lord." Comes a
contradiction or a thorn: "It is the Lord!" Comes a joy, a
pleasure: "It is he, I recognize him everywhere! I see nothing any more but him: *Dominus est!* Jesus, you may hide
yourself behind secondary causes, behind creatures: you will
not fool me. I shall always recognize you."

There existed between Jesus and John the particular tenderness which comes from preference. Jesus had a special

tenderness for John. And John knew himself to be preferred. There was between the gentle Master and himself a special atmosphere, something different, sacred. John was quick to understand his divine Friend. One look told him more than twenty words to the others. He perceived better than all the rest what made him suffer, what consoled him. He had those intuitions which are the exclusive privilege of intimacy. The most intimate movements of the heart of Jesus always found their echo in the heart of John. So Jesus gave him his mother. He confided her to his care. John believed that he was loved—and this was the secret of his love. "And I, I believed in love!" "*Et nos credidimus caritati!*" I knew love and I believed in love!

Why was St. John the preferred, the beloved at the Cenacle, the evangelist of love *par excellence*, the seer of Patmos? He tells us in a word: "Because I believed in love."

All his marvelous, ineffable story he explains in those few words. It was the love of St. John for Jesus that permitted him to see the Word of Life. He tells us: "That which was from the beginning, which we have heard, which we have seen with our eyes, which we have looked upon and our hands have handled, of the word of life" *(1 Jn 1:1)*. And he makes the supreme revelation: *Deus caritas est.* "God is love" *(1 Jn 4:8)*.

How do you learn that God is love? By your intimacy with Jesus. Where do you learn to live in this intimacy? At the foot of the tabernacle, at the Mass, and in the gospel. It is there that Jesus reveals himself to us, in his words, in his acts, his whole Heart, and all the attributes of his love. It is there that we can understand with St. Paul and all the saints, the width, the breadth, the height, the depth of his infinite charity. Father Loew, in his admirable book entitled *As If He Saw the Invisible,*[2] states forcefully, "The Christian life will never be anything other than a friendship of man with God;" and if there is a definition of charity to which we must constantly come back, as to the source of our youth and wonder, it is certainly that of St. Thomas Aquinas:

"Charity is friendship with God." Truly Jesus speaks to us as to friends.

"As the Father has loved me, I also have loved you. Abide in my love. . . . These things I have spoken to you that my joy may be in you, and your joy may be filled. This is my commandment, that you love one another, as I have loved you. . . . You are my friends . . . because all things, whatsoever I have heard of my Father, I have made known to you. You have not chosen me, but I have chosen you" *(Jn 15:9, 11, 15, 16).*

"Let not your heart be troubled. You believe in God: believe also in me. In my Father's house there are many mansions. If not, I would have told you: because I go to prepare a place for you. And if I shall go and prepare a place for you, I will come again and will take you to myself: that where I am, you also may be. And whither I go you know: and the way you know. . . . I am the way and the truth, and the life" *(Jn 14:1-3, 6).*

Has a friend ever spoken with such tenderness to a friend? These are phenomenal words. See this need he had to share with his friends, to share his joy and his glory, to be loved of the Father, to share his table in his Kingdom. "I go to prepare a place for you." The need of friends to be together: "Father, I will that where I am they also whom you have given me may be with me" *(Jn 17:24).*

I have found admirable responses of living faith to these words of Jesus in the parting words of three persons at the moment of death: of Charles Maurras, a deaf man, who said, "For the first time I hear someone coming;" of Gaby Morlay, the actress, who said, "I am not going away, I am arriving;" and still more profoundly, of a little black man who said, "I am going home." He understood it all. How I wish for all of you at the moment of death to say, "I am going home."

Read and reread the texts of the Council. With an exalted tone, a gravity, a serenity, in which we can sense the breath of the Holy Spirit, they teach us the truth, they enlarge the life in us.

"The Lord," says the Council, "is the goal of human history, the focal point of the longings of history and of civilization, the center of the human race, the joy of every heart and the answer to all its yearnings. He it is whom the Father raised from the dead, lifted on high and stationed at his right hand, making Him Judge of the living and the dead. Enlivened and united in His Spirit, we journey toward the consummation of human history, one which fully accords with the counsel of God's love: 'To re-establish all things in Christ, both those in the heavens and those on the earth.' "[3]

And Paul VI: "We shall never have finished plumbing the mystery of the personality of Jesus. We shall never have finished listening to him as Master, imitating him as an example, loving him as Savior. We shall never have finished discovering his relevance, his importance for all the great questions of our times; we shall never have finished sensing the birth in us, as a unique spiritual experience, of the desire, the torment, the hope to be able finally to see him, to meet him, to understand and taste to the point of supreme happiness, that he is our new and true life and our salvation."[4]

"We must live in the hope of meeting Jesus as we meet a travelling pilgrim on the way, a friend we know, a brother of our own blood, a Master of our own tongue, a liberator who can accomplish everything, a Savior."[5]

Voices among the bishops are heard, saying in a similar way, "The Church, open to the world, is the Heart of Christ open once for all on the Cross; the Heart from which flow the blood and water of salvation, the Heart never closed, in order to draw in all men in the love of God. There is no other openness of the Church to the world."[6]

Ever since the fall we have been profoundly marked by fear, and we retain in our depths the vision of the angel brandishing his flashing sword to bar our way to the tree of life *(cf. Gn 3:24)*, as if, since then, there had not been Bethlehem, the sweetness of Nazareth, the Redemption of Calvary, the ineffable gift of the Eucharist, the total victory of the Resurrection.

Someone asked me at the end of one retreat, "But are we then nothing?" This cry moved me. On the contrary, you are the man of whom the Psalmist said:

"What is man that you are mindful of him? . . . You have made him a little less than the angels: you have crowned him with glory and honor, and have set him over the works of your hands. You have subjected all things under his feet" *(Ps 8:5-7)*.

"Fear not, for I have redeemed you, and called you by your name. You are mine. . . . Since you became honorable in my eyes, you are glorious. I have loved you: and I will give men for you, and people for your life" *(Is 43:1;4)*.

You are also the man to whom the Spirit speaks in the Apocalypse:

"You say: I am rich and made wealthy and have need of nothing: and know not that you are wretched and miserable and poor and blind and naked. I counsel you to buy of me gold, fire-tried, that you may be made rich and may be clothed in white garments: and that the shame of your nakedness may not appear. And anoint your eyes with eye salve, that you may see" *(Ap 3:17, 18)*.

Is it not good to be a poor man made rich, a blind man made to see, a prisoner made free, a condemned man granted mercy, much more a sinner pardoned and raised to divine life?

I have often thought, during my talks to you, about the comment that Maurice Maignan, one of the first companions of Ozanam, made after a retreat: "One thought strikes me. All the means of sanctification which the preacher proposes and develops require a strong soul. . . . I will not profit from exercises designed for strong souls. O my God, show me the exercises designed for feeble souls. Would the saints have forgotten or disdained them? Yet even if the saints did not think of these poor souls, who are nevertheless most numerous, you, Lord, my mercy, have not abandoned them. You yourself, Good Master, have burdened yourself with them. I know that better than anyone. I am one of those souls and I bless you for having revealed to the weak and the little ones what you do not always accord to the valiant and the strong."[7]

Here we come back to the star of our retreat, little St. Thérèse, of whom Father Philipon thinks that "her influence is destined to dominate modern spirituality for several centuries, carrying a new message to men of our times."[8]

Here again we find the profound moral theology of St. Paul:

"I am content with my infirmities, reproaches, necessities, my persecutions and distresses, for the sake of Christ. For when I am weak, then am I strong" *(2 Cor 12:10)*.

· "I can do all things in him who strengthens me" *(Phil 4:13)*.

Do not let yourself be influenced by the accusations of sentimentalism, of dolorism, of outmoded individualism, brought against those who do not fear to speak about the Heart of Jesus and the Heart of Mary. You cannot go wrong by following St. Gertrude, St. Francis de Sales, St. Margaret Mary, St. Thérèse of the Child Jesus, and the popes—all echoes of St. John.

No! The Holy Church has not been a tree in winter up until Vatican II, giving no leaves or flowers or fruits until now.

One of the expressions of thanks after a retreat which has given me the most supernatural joy is this: "You have preached to us the eternal truths of all ages."

There is nothing in the world of which I am more sure than I am of the love of Jesus for each one of us. There is nothing which I affirm with more assurance to a soul than the fact that Jesus loves each of us to the point of the foolishness of the Cross and the glory of the Resurrection.

You must repeat again and again, to believing and unbelieving souls, in awaiting his return, that Jesus loves them. Repeat again and again the message of the Christmas angel: "I bring you tidings of great joy: a Savior is born unto you." And finally, you must believe in Love.

Chapter 1

1. Message at Lisieux, July 11, 1954.
2. The *Exultet*.
3. St. Thérèse's Act of Offering.
4. *Novissima Verba*, p. 37.
5. Cf. Apostolic letter, *Inde a primis*, June 30, 1960.
6. *Novissima Verba*, p. 190.
7. *Manuscrits autobiographiques de St. Thérèse de l'E.J.*, p. 183.
8. *Novissima Verba*, p. 112.

Chapter 2

1. Council of Trent, Session VI, Chapter IX.
2. *Manuscrits autobiographiques*, p. 244.
3. St. Augustine, *Etymology*.
4. *Summa Theologica*, II to II 9, 30.
5. *Manuscrits autobiographiques*, p. 313.
6. *Novissima Verba*, p. 61.
7. *Histoire d'une Ame*, p. 266.
8. *Manuscrits autobiographiques*, p. 237
9. *Manuscrits autobiographiques*, p. 233.
10. Letter of July 18, 1893.
11. Letter of June 6, 1897.
12. Letter of September 17, 1896.
13. *Manuscrits autobiographiques*, p. 211.
14. *Novissima Verba*, p. 93.

Chapter 3

1. Abbé Nodet, *J. M. Vianney* (Ed. Xavier Mappus), p. 132.
2. *Manuscrits autobiographiques*, p. 235.
3. Letter of April 26, 1889.
4. Letter of Christmas, 1896.
5. Letter of May 28, 1897.
6. *Manuscrits autobiographiques*, p. 186.
7. *Novissima Verba*, p. 97.
8. *Manuscrits autobiographiques*, p. 189.
9. *Novissima Verba*, p. 139.
10. *Manuscrits autobiographiques*, p. 248.
11. Testimony of Sister Genevieve of the Holy Face.
12. Discourse on August 14, 1921.
13. Discourses of May 17 and 18, 1925, and April 30, 1923.
14. Message of July 11, 1954.
15. *Annales de Lisieux*, July 1963, p. 3.
16. *Manuscrits autobiographiques*, p. 227.
17. Letter of September 17, 1896.
18. *Manuscrits autobiographiques*, p. 209.
19. Letter of May 9, 1897.
20. St. Thérèse's Act of Offering.
21. *Histoire d'une Ame*, p. 281.

22. *Manuscrits autobiographiques,* pp. 250 and 253.
23. Letter of April 1890.
24. Nodet, *J. M. Vianney,* p. 132.
25. Letter of September 17, 1896.

Chapter 4

1. *Summa Theologica,* III s.9.73, art. 3.
2. *Manuscrits autobiographiques,* p. 237.
3. Letter 133.
4. *Manuscrits autobiographique,* p. 207.
5. *Histoire d'une Ame,* p. 238.
6. "Seventh Mansion" in St. Teresa's *Interior Castle.*
7. *Novissima Verba,* p. 125.
8. *Confessions* (tr. by F. J. Sheed, Sheed & Ward, New York, 1943), Book V, p. 93.
9. Act of thanksgiving after Mass.
10. Pierre de Caussade, *L'abandon à la Providence divine* (Ed. Y. Gabalda), pp. 1, 109, 11, 7, 20.

Chapter 5

1. In July, 1954.
2. Letter of September 17, 1896.
3. *Histoire d'une Ame,* p. 284.

Chapter 6

1. *Manuscrits autobiographiques,* pp. 266 and 264.
2. *Ibid.* pp. 297, 298.
3. *Esprit de Ste Thérèse de l'E.J.,* p. 84.
4. St. John Chrysostom, Homily 18 on 2 Corinthians.

Chapter 7

1. Discourse of April 12, 1964.
2. Records of the Mother House.
3. *Vie,* by Msgr. Laveille, p. 366.
4. Apostolic Brief of May 3, 1944.
5. *Pie XI et son Etoile,* p. 43.
6. Letter of August 15, 1892.
7. *Vie par ses contemporains,* Vol. 1, p. 159.
8. *Pacem in terris,* no. 168.
9. February 2, 1961.
10. Discourse of August 21, 1929.
11. St. Catherine of Siena.
12. *Manuscrits autobiographiques,* p. 227.
13. *Novissima Verba,* pp. 78 and 60.
14. Read the encouraging details of this incident in the life of the Curé of Ars, St. John Vianney (Ed. Vitte-1929), by Msgr. Trochu, p. 631.

Chapter 8

1. *Manuscrits autobiographiques*, p. 177.
2. *Novissima Verba*, p. 136.
3. *Esprit de Ste. Thérèse de l'E.J.*, p. 108.
4. *Notes intimes* (Ed. Stock), p. 265.
5. *Summa Theologica*, III 9.46 a. 3.
6. *La Rédemption par le sang*, by Father Philippe of the Trinity.
7. *La Resurrection de Jésus, mystère de salut.*

Chapter 9

1. Vatican II: Constitution on the Sacred Liturgy, 47.
2. Pius XII, *Mediator Dei*, nos. 67-69.
3. Secret of the Ninth Sunday after Pentecost, Roman Missal.
4. *Lumen Gentium*, 10.
5. Pius XII, *Mediator Dei*, 103, 105, 109.
6. *Manuscrits autobiographiques*, p. 210.
7. *Ibid.* p. 229.
8. *Ibid.*, p. 307.
9. St. Leo the Great, Sermon 637.
10. Dom Marmion, *Le Christ dans ses mystères*, p. 132.
11. *Manuscrits autobiographiques*, pp. 199 & 117.
12. Hymn by St. Thomas Aquinas.
13. *Manuscrits autobiographiques*, p. 312.
14. *Ibid.*, p. 290.
15. *Ibid.*, p. 200.
16. *Ibid.*, p. 200.
17. *Ibid.*, p. 209.
18. It has also an "external auxiliary" to which all are admitted who desire to live in the spirit of the congregation.
19. *Vie et oeuvres du Père Mateo*, Fathers of the Sacred Hearts of Picpus, 108 avenue de la Republique, 91 Montegeron.
20. *Decree on the Apostolate of the Laity*, 11.
21. *The Church in the Modern World*, 48: par. 8.
22. *Decree on the Apostolate of the Laity*, 4.
23. *Pensées et conseils apostoliques du Père Mateo*, pp. 11 and 17.

Chapter 10

1. Cf. *Lumen Gentium*, 62.
2. *Comme s'il voyait l'invisible*, p. 43.
3. *The Church in the Modern World*, no. 45.
4. Discourse of February 1, 1967.
5. Christmas Message, 1965.
6. Cardinal Renard, *L'esprit du Concile.*
7. *Maurice Maignan*, Vol. II, p. 1287.
8. M. Philipon, *Une vie toute nouvelle*, p. 17.